The philatelists.

ABERDEEN PHILATELIC SOCIETY 1910-2010

A History of Philately in Northeast Scotland

Jeffrey C. Stone

Aberdeen Philatelic Society

Published in 2010 by the Aberdeen Philatelic Society

Copyright © Aberdeen Philatelic Society

ISBN 978 0 9509891 1 2

Printed by Aberdeen University Central Printing Service

Frontispiece: Mr I Smillie (right) and Mr A S Mackie, c.1955

Front cover: above – a cover addressed to founder member Edmund Bell at his office where the Society was inaugurated in 1910; below – a cover commemorating a stamp exhibition in Aberdeen in 1948.

LOTTERY FUNDED

AaM15

FOREWORD

Collecting satisfies an ancient need, providing an atavistic link to our hunter-gatherer past. We do not have to gather basic necessities, they are provided by trade within our complex society. Yet within twenty years or so of Sir Rowland Hill's invention of the postage stamp "a label backed by a glutinous wash that may be affixed to a letter to show that the cost of conveyance had been paid", enough countries had copied Great Britain's example to allow the emergence of the stamp collector, who wanted one of each, followed by dealers and their listings.

The public image of the "Stamp Collector" is of an elderly person, usually male with glasses, peering at a stamp through a magnifying glass. This may have been reinforced by the fact that both King George V and Franklin D. Roosevelt found refuge from their public work in their collections. Stamp collecting or philately as it became, appeals to all, male, female, young and old.

Just as the original hunter-gatherers came together and evolved, so did the first stamp collectors come together in the first philatelic societies. Dr Stone's book describes how this happened here in Aberdeen from the first very formal meetings in 1910 through to the thriving, much less formal group that is the Aberdeen Philatelic Society approaching its centenary.

As in society at large, fashions have changed in stamp collecting and whilst all our members have stamp collections, they also have knowledge of the details of postage stamp production and the reasons behind issued stamps, which identifies them as philatelists, a word coined to mean "a lover of exemption from payment", in this case postage. Some have interests in the themes or subject of the stamp, *thematics,* or perhaps the study of early airmails and their stamps, *aero philately.* Others are interested in the posts themselves, how they evolved in response to the challenges of geography or war, *postal history.*

The Aberdeen Philatelic Society has found a diligent biographer in Dr Stone who shows how this came about and added to the social fabric of Aberdeen in a book which will be of interest to philatelists, philatelic societies, social and local historians.

A.D. Kindley FRPSL
President, Aberdeen Philatelic Society.

PREFACE

In the introduction to his monumental account of *The Royal Philatelic Collection* (1952), Sir John Wilson suggested that "the history of [stamp] collecting is very little understood". More than half a century on, it is probably still true to say that the history of the hobby has not been thoroughly researched. Some major biographical and bibliographical studies have been published in recent years but philatelic historiography remains scanty in some aspects. How has the hobby evolved over a century and a half? Wilson pointed to changes in attitudes towards rarity and condition. The preferred subject matter of collectors has evidently changed through the decades, as has the way in which they have built and displayed their collections, but can we be more specific? How have the institutions of philately changed? There are surely discernible shifts in the topics which philatelists have chosen for study and research? In what way do the collectors of the past differ from today's adherents to the hobby? Do we have any idea of how many collectors there were in the past and how many there are today? Has the status of the hobby changed through time?

A current trend suggests that the history of the hobby as it has been practised in the United Kingdom may be about to become a little better documented, albeit in a rather indirect way. A number of British philatelic societies have already reached their centennial and others will do so shortly. Some mark the occasion by publishing a postal history of their locality. Others have chosen to place on record the history of their own society and in so doing, contributed perforce to the recorded history of philately. A narrative history of the Aberdeen Philatelic Society is a record of evolution and change in the way that the members have pursued their hobby over the decades. It is also a record of change in the conduct and management of the Society and in its relationship to the institutional hierarchy of organised philately. These changes are, no doubt, more widely representative. Hence, this account is offered both as a celebration of a century of organised philately in Aberdeen and as a modest contribution to the history of the hobby.

The Aberdeen and North of Scotland PS was the fourth philatelic society to come into being in Scotland, following the Scottish PS, the Dundee and District PS and the Junior PS of Scotland. The minutes of the inaugural meeting were written in copper-plate, in a stout ledger, thus setting a high standard of record keeping which has been maintained for a century. The minutes of every subsequent formal meeting of the Society remain intact. They are a detailed record and are the main source for this account, despite occasional inconsistencies, for example, in the content of reports by office bearers at annual general meetings. They are, nevertheless, a remarkably complete and full record, perhaps most remarkable for the fact that no less than twenty-one Secretaries, past and present, have all been meticulous in maintaining the written record of the Society's business. In addition, the Society's archive contains a large number of photographs, press cuttings and printed ephemera, whilst the Society's excellent library has also been a valuable source of information.

I would like to acknowledge the assistance of Aberdeen Library and Information Services, Aberdeen City Archives; Special Libraries and Archives, University of Aberdeen; the Librarian, Royal Philatelic Society London, as well as the membership of the Society, especially B. Walker, A.L. Walker, A.S. Mackie, G. McD. Mackintosh, A. D. Kindley, N. Lutwyche, I.B. Kennaway, D.A. Macdonald and Mrs S. Den. I am also grateful for the assistance of philatelists elsewhere in Scotland, including S. Gardiner, A.D. Shepherd and A.H. Watson. I am especially grateful for the drafting and proof-reading skills of my wife Margaret.

Aberdeen Philatelic Society gratefully acknowledges the financial assistance of the British Philatelic Trust and Awards for All Scotland in meeting the costs of this publication.

Jeffrey C. Stone FRPSL,
June 2009.

CONTENTS

Chapter 1

In the Beginning

On Wednesday 30th March 1910, nine philatelists assembled in the Union Street offices of W. Edmund Bell, Solicitor. The minutes of the meeting suggest that the business was conducted in a very formal manner, reflecting the contemporary social context. Mr James Anderson was called to the chair and expressed the view that interest in stamp collecting had reached a point when a local society could be formed to good purpose. He pointed out that while some in the town were advanced collectors, "there were many more who were quite novices and who would gain great benefit from the opportunity of sitting at the feet of some philatelic Gamaliel[1]", to quote the minutes.

James Anderson, FRPSL, President 1910-20. [*Photo: Bon Accord, 1912.*]

---

[1] Acts 22, 3.

Mr Edward Alexander then invited the meeting to confirm the sentiments expressed by the Chair, by proposing a motion "that it is of the opinion of this meeting that it is desirable to form a Society in Aberdeen and the North of Scotland to promote the collection and study of postage stamps". Mr Bell then moved "that in accordance with the foregoing resolution, this meeting do now form itself into the Society, and that the terms of this and the previous resolution be communicated through the press and by circular to philatelists and stamp collectors residing in Aberdeen and the North of Scotland and that the Society be called "The Aberdeen and North of Scotland Philatelic Society". Office bearers and committee members were then appointed, a subscription was set and it was decided that the Society should meet every third Wednesday from October to March. Perhaps the most interesting phrase in the carefully-worded second resolution was the conscious differentiation between "philatelists and stamp collectors"!

The inauguration of the Society on 30 March was reported locally in the *Aberdeen Free Press* and more widely in the philatelic press, in *The Postage Stamp*, *Gibbon's Stamp Weekly* and the *Congress Handbook*. The *Free Press* report is a more expansive record of the Chairman's remarks, saying that their hobby needed no apology and continuing:

> "To outsiders philately is a mysterious cult, as they know nothing of its educative, scientific or recreational value. By their presence they indicated their allegiance to the army of old gums or the King's head party, and he hoped they had come prepared to march forward with the progressive spirit of the age, in forming a philatelic society in Aberdeen. Dundee could boast of its flourishing philatelic society, and he saw no reason why Aberdeen should continue to burn its philatelic candles under bushels."[2]

---

[2] *Aberdeen Free Press*, 2 April 1910, 4.

A Philatelic Society for Aberdeen

An Enthusiastic and Successful Meeting

AT a meeting of local stamp collectors, held in the offices of Mr. W. Edmund Bell, Solicitor, Union Street, this week, the advisability of forming a local philatelic society was discussed says the *Aberdeen Free Press* (2.4.10). There was a good attendance, presided over by Mr. James Anderson, others who were present, or who expressed a desire that such a society should be formed being Messrs. Edward Alexander, J.P.S.: W. Edmund Bell,

He then called on Mr. Edward Alexander, who proposed the following motion—That it is the opinion of this meeting that it is desirable to form a society in Aberdeen and the north of Scotland to promote the collection and study of postage stamps. This motion was unanimously carried.

Mr. W. Edmund Bell then moved—That, in accordance with the foregoing resolution, this meeting do now form itself into the society, and

The inaugural meeting was reported in a weekly philatelic journal.

Two weeks later, the committee met for the first time to draft the Constitution of the Society. This was adopted at a General Meeting of the Society on 21 April 1910, when the Secretary was instructed to draw up a programme of meetings. The Society had come into being, although to quote a press report of the 50th anniversary celebrations in 1960, "there was a collectors' club of some sort before the society was formed in 1910". There seems to be no other record of this forerunner club, apart from a cryptic posthumous reference to the first President as someone "who organised and privately publicised this Society before it was publicly publicised in 1910". An earlier more informal group sounds entirely plausible in view of the presence of a number of active collectors of long-standing in Aberdeen.

The new committee was clearly energetic. The first syllabus, printed and hard-bound, sets out a programme of twelve meetings for session 1910-11, together with the "Articles of Constitution" and a list of twenty-eight members. Throughout the first session decisions were taken on a range of issues, as the Society developed. At the first meeting the Society decided to join The Postage Stamp League, a national society established in 1910 to promote and popularise stamp collecting by means of the loan of "lantern lectures" and by circulating informative pamphlets to schools[3]. It seems that the committee had actually taken the decision to join by May 1910, when the Aberdeen Society is recorded as the third society to join. At the third meeting, the Society admitted the wife of the President as an honorary member, the first lady member. The conduct of meetings evidently lead to a suggestion that occasional informal meetings be arranged so that members could become better acquainted. At the fourth meeting it was decided that no dealers be admitted as members of the Society meantime. At the first Annual General Meeting the Society admitted a Mrs Irvine, Peterhead, as the first lady member in her own right, and following that meeting, members adjourned to the Palace Hotel for the first annual dinner.

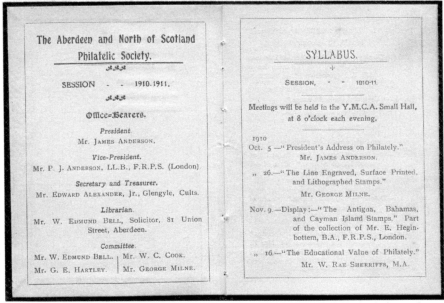

The first syllabus was hard-bound and included the Articles of Constitution, Members 1910-11, and Membership Card.

---

[3] [Melville, F.J.], 1910, "The Postage Stamp League", *The Postage Stamp* 6, 2, 14-15 & 6, 7, 81.

Chapter 2

A Suitable Place to Meet

A regular programme of meetings is usually the predominant activity of any locally-based philatelic society. The search for an appropriate venue for meetings is a recurring item on Aberdeen PS committee agendas over the years, as circumstances changed. The determinants are capacity, accessibility, cost, storage space, lighting, comfort and, of course, availability. These factors evolved and changed over the decades, resulting in frequent searches for new venues.

In 1910 the committee accepted an invitation to hold their first season of meetings in the solicitor's offices where they were convened. In fact, the Society met for the first time on 5 October 1910 in the YMCA Small Hall. Why the committee changed its mind is not recorded. Numbers attending in that first season averaged 18, excluding the AGM, so perhaps the need was for a larger venue.

For the first meeting of the 1911-12 season, the society met in the Library of Aberdeen University's recently opened Marischal College. The reason may have been that the first meeting that season was addressed by the University's illustrious Librarian and philatelic historian, P.J. Anderson, who spoke on "Notes on Early Philatelic Literature with Illustrations from Aberdeen University Library". It was, presumably, more convenient to meet in University precincts than to transport Library stock to an outside venue. What may have been an experimental venue was utilised for the rest of the season, not in the Library but in the Agriculture Lecture Room, perhaps arranged by J. McLauchlan Young, a founder member who was also Lecturer in Veterinary Hygiene at the University. The Sacrist received an honorarium of £1 for his pains! At the AGM the membership voted to remain in Marischal College, in preference to the YMCA, and the Society remained there for the next two seasons. At the AGM in 1914 "a vote of thanks was accorded to the University Authorities for the use of the room in Marischal College".

One can but wonder whether costs were waived under the benign influence of the University Librarian.

The schedule of meetings was severely disrupted in 1914 by the outbreak of war. The three meetings which were convened in 1914-15 and the four meetings in the following season all took place in Marischal College, when numbers attending dropped to single figures. Three informal meetings were arranged for 1916-17, with the venue removed to 35a Union Street, the office of the Secretary, who received a donation of ten shillings "for light and rooms". Not even that modest venue was required for 1917-18, since it was decided that no meetings should be held that season "owing to the continuance of the war", a situation which appears to have continued through 1918-19.

The climate had understandably changed by the AGM of March 1919, when it was remitted to the committee "to look out a room for the use of the Society at a rent not exceeding twelve pounds per annum". The committee hired the Basement Room in the YMCA. The Society grew rapidly in the next few years and there was frequent discussion of alternative venues, including a return to Marischal College. In 1920-21 the Society moved to the Central School, Belmont Street. Next season they moved again, to the East United Free Church, Schoolhill, before returning to the Parlour of the YMCA for three seasons. In 1925-26 they moved yet again for three seasons, this time to the Radio Society Rooms, 259 Union Street.

A remarkable proposal was made at the AGM of 1920, when a member suggested "a permanent Room for the Society" and "the matter was remitted to the Housing Committee to make enquiries and report". Little is known of that committee or of its deliberations. No further mention of the proposal is recorded until the first meeting of 1928, when it was intimated that two suitable rooms at 29 Adelphi were available and the matter was referred to the committee. A sub-committee was rapidly set up "to proceed with the question of acquiring the rooms". A rental agreement was entered into and on 1 February 1928, the Secretary was instructed to obtain linoleum and chairs, "at a cost not to exceed 3/- per chair". Funds were gifted for the purchase of furniture and arrangements quickly made for the installation of gas and electricity meters and gas fires. Within a month, linoleum had been laid and the Secretary's authorisation for the purchase of chairs had risen to 5/-, so that new chairs could be acquired, rather than second hand.

On 14 March 1928 the Society held an opening meeting in its new rooms in the Adelphi. The President welcomed a large gathering, declaring that the Society was the nearest that it had yet been to being permanently housed, presumably a reference to their peripatetic existence in recent years. The rooms were formally declared open by the first President of the Society, James Anderson, who "traced at considerable length and detail the formation and development of the Society since its inception", followed by an interval for tea! Thereafter, Edmund Bell delivered a paper on "The Hobby" and invited the visitors to enrol as members.

Three months after the opening, the committee was summoned to approve a proposal for letting the front room for financial reasons, the back room being sufficient for the needs of the Society. Within months, a Mr Ral, jeweller, was occupying one of the rooms, but by 1934, the Society had grown to such an extent that a sub-committee was appointed to try to find larger rooms. It was not successful and a year later, a further sub-committee was appointed with the same remit, but to no avail. By 1937 "discomfort due to lack of space" was the cause of the decision to terminate the lease of rooms in the Adelphi and the venue for the Society's meetings in 1937-38 became the Caledonian Hotel. There was a record attendance of seventy members at the first meeting of the season, held in "a very comfortable meeting room", according to the visiting speaker. At the conclusion, members were invited to tender for the Society's furniture.

After only one season at the Caledonian Hotel, the Society removed once again, this time to the Loyal Order of Ancient Shepherds' Halls,[4] 42 Union Terrace, where it remained for five years, although there is no record of formal meetings in the 1939-40 and 1940-41 seasons. "The Second World War...put a stop to all conventional social practices except perhaps that of drinking".[5] By 1942 there was a return to normality in the form of a regular schedule of meetings, which in turn lead to a call for more comfortable surroundings. These were found for the 1943-44 and the subsequent season at the Institute of Bankers' Rooms, 375 Union Street, followed by a further move to the Caledonian Order of United Oddfellows' Hall, 15 Belmont Street in 1945. By 1949 the Oddfellows' Hall was too small and a new venue was found in the Round Room of the Music Hall, Union Street, where meetings continued until 1952, when the factor of cost brought about a move to the adjacent YMCA.

Thereafter changes in venue were much less frequent. The Society met in the YMCA for twenty years, apart from one meeting in 1963 when the YMCA declined to make the usual meeting room available and the Society met instead in the Victoria Restaurant, Union Street. The Secretary sent a strong letter of protest to the YMCA! Evidently not everyone was happy with the YMCA. In 1965 there was debate about alternative venues in the context of concern over declining numbers of members attending meetings. One member delivered "a long tirade of the poor and noisy conditions". Attendance did pick up in 1966-67, but the decision to move was finally taken in 1971, following continuing dissatisfaction over noise and also lighting.

In 1971-72 the Society convened in the YWCA, Bon Accord Square, resulting in immediate complaints of poor lighting. Two rooms were occasionally utilised in the new venue, but in December 1973 a

---

[4] The LOAS was a nation-wide friendly society founded in 1827, providing sickness benefit and funeral expenses.

[5] Keith, Alexander, 1972, *A Thousand Years of Aberdeen*, Aberdeen UP, 530.

problem not specific to the venue brought about the cancellation of meetings. The energy crisis meant that the rooms could not be heated and meetings were cancelled until further notice, in fact, until March 1974. By 1977 the use of display frames was under consideration, but their storage would present a problem at the current venue. The Arts Centre, King Street, was seriously considered, but the solution was found, as well as the resolution of the problem of poor lighting, in a new venue on the other side of Bon Accord Square, in the Northern Arts Club, where the Society met for the first time in 1978-79 season and remained for a further twenty seasons.

It was perhaps a reflection of the age-profile of the membership that a change of venue was debated in 1999. Two steep flights of stairs as well as shortage of car parking were proving increasingly onerous and the Friday morning group had already found an attractive alternative in the newly-built Rubislaw Church Centre, Fountainhall Road. The Society removed to this venue in 1999-2000 and has continued to enjoy the excellent facilities subsequently. The location is relatively convenient, the lighting is excellent, there is a lift to the first floor, there is storage space for the library and for the frames, and refreshment facilities are available. The attractive venue has probably been a contributory factor in the very good attendances at meetings in recent years.

The Society has convened in some twenty different locations over its lifetime, if occasional rearrangements are included.

The President opens an evening meeting in relaxed fashion, in the Society's current venue.

Chapter 3

An Evolving Programme of Meetings

The programmes of meetings organiscd by the committee for the first two years of the Society's existence seem to reflect the educational role which had been advanced, with a biblical reference, as a prime reason for the formation of the Society. That purpose was to allow the novice to benefit from the experienced philatelist. The syllabus for the first two years thus included evenings devoted to printing methods, paper making, colour, perforation and the arranging and mounting of a collection. These meetings seem to have been discursive, with an introductory lecture or "paper". Other meetings were spccifically designated as "Displays". There were only four such nights in the very first season, when all of the displays (of different parts of the West Indies) were from the collection of J.E. Heginbottom of Rochdale, a frequent contributor to the philatelic press, of whom it is stated that "portions of his collection have been displayed before almost every Philatelic Society in Gt. Britain, of most of which he is a member"[6]. The displays were sent to the Society for display, together with accompanying papers which were read.

While membership remained small, the educational function was presumably quickly fulfilled. By the third and fourth season displays of stamps and the participation of the membership are more evident, although themes rather than countries predominate. There are evenings devoted to Designs, Rowland Hill, King George V Stamps, Triangular Stamps, even Ugly Stamps! "Lantern Illustrations" are occasionally used. One member began to create a name for himself as the author of light-hearted philatelic poetry which was recited at

---

[6] *Who's Who in Philately*, London, 1914, 52.

meetings and frequently published in the local press under the title of Philatelic Frivolities[7].

The very first full meeting on 5 October 1910 was fully reported in next day's *Evening Express*, with a seemingly beneficial effect on attendance at subsequent meetings that session, but attendance at meetings for the first four seasons rarely exceeded twenty. In 1913 a Society meeting of general interest was advertised in the *Aberdeen Journal* and the *Aberdeen Free Press*, but the outbreak of war resulted in a severe curtailment of meetings, most of them devoted to war stamps, except for AGMs. Attendances were also severely depleted.

On the resumption of a normal syllabus in 1919, the topics chosen were again aspects or themes, including instructional topics such as stamp papers, postmarks, watermarks and question nights, with relatively few evenings specifically devoted to displays of the stamps of named countries. The presentation of these topics is perhaps characterised in a report in the *Aberdeen Daily Journal* of the address to the Society by John Anderson on 2 February 1921, entitled "A Chat on Postage Stamps", in which he compared philately today with some twenty years previously.

The 1919 syllabus invited members to contribute to the displays at all meetings, so presumably the stamps of many countries were laid before meetings. There is a hint in the record of the AGM of 1923 that members wanted to see more stamps at meetings. Among eight suggestions recorded, four propose new forms of displays at meetings. Nevertheless, the predominance of aspects of philately over countries, with the notable exception of Great Britain, continued in programmes until the late 1920s, when a distinct change in

---

[7] See John Thomson, Jr. [in] *Bon Accord*, 1912-13, a founder of the journal and described as "a born humorist to extract so much fun from so barren, prosaic and serious an occupation as stamp collecting". The Society library retains a bound volume of fifty of his published doggerel verses (see chapter 13).

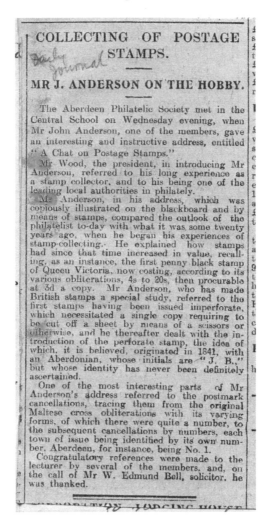

COLLECTING OF POSTAGE STAMPS.

MR J. ANDERSON ON THE HOBBY.

The Aberdeen Philatelic Society met in the Central School on Wednesday evening, when Mr John Anderson, one of the members, gave an interesting and instructive address, entitled "A Chat on Postage Stamps."

Mr Wood, the president, in introducing Mr Anderson, referred to his long experience as a stamp collector, and to his being one of the leading local authorities in philately.

Mr Anderson, in his address, which was copiously illustrated on the blackboard and by means of stamps, compared the outlook of the philatelist to-day with what it was some twenty years ago, when he began his experiences of stamp-collecting. He explained how stamps had since that time increased in value, recalling, as an instance, the first penny black stamp of Queen Victoria, now costing, according to its various obliterations, 4s to 20s, then procurable at 3d a copy. Mr Anderson, who has made British stamps a special study, referred to the first stamps having been issued imperforate, which necessitated a single copy requiring to be cut off a sheet by means of a scissors or otherwise, and he thereafter dealt with the introduction of the perforate stamp, the idea of which, it is believed, originated in 1841, with an Aberdonian, whose initials are "J. B.," but whose identity has never been definitely ascertained.

One of the most interesting parts of Mr Anderson's address referred to the postmark cancellations, tracing them from the original Maltese cross obliterations with its varying forms, of which there were quite a number, to the subsequent cancellations by numbers, each town of issue being identified by its own number. Aberdeen, for instance, being No. 1.

Congratulatory references were made to the lecturer by several of the members, and, on the call of Mr W. Edmund Bell, solicitor, he was thanked.

Press report of the meeting of 2 February 1921

emphasis occurs in the balance of annual programmes, with a larger proportion of the programmes now given over to invited displays of named stamp-issuing authorities.

In 1920 the then President suggested that a "popular philatelist from the South" be invited to lecture to the Society on its opening night, as a "means of stirring up enthusiasm thereby augmenting membership". Fred J. Melville, President of the JPS, London, accepted the invitation for an out-of-pocket fee of £12.12/-. His public lecture on "Old Classics", illustrated with lantern slides, was advertised in the *Evening Express* and took place in the Ball Room of the Music Hall on 13 October 1920, admission 1/6 for Adults and 6d for Juniors. The Marquis of Aberdeen and Temair presided. A synopsis of his lecture shows that the first half of his talk was devoted to the stamps of Great Britain and the second part to foreign and colonial stamps. There was said to be a good attendance of members and friends. This bold initiative gave rise to a deficit on the Melville account almost equal to his fee!

In 1921 the Society approached the Dundee and District PS to no avail, suggesting an exchange of displays, a first move towards Society visits which were eventually to become a regular feature of the syllabus. In 1922, however, the President of the Dundee Society, Dr A.E. Kidd, gave a display of Serbia to the Society, an occasion which was seen as the forerunner for exchanges of speakers between the two societies. That same year Charles Wilson travelled from Aberdeen to display Hawaii to the Dundee Society. The following season several members from Aberdeen visited Dundee in the context of Dr Kidd's initiative in promoting joint meetings of Scottish societies (see Ch. 15), but a visit by six members of the Dundee society to Aberdeen was also arranged outside the scheduled programme of Society meetings for the 1922-23 season. The function took place in the Imperial Hotel and displays were followed by a formal dinner with an appropriate list of toasts and a drole "menu philatelique" offering such culinary delights as "Watermarks turned

STAMPS OF THE OLDEN DAYS.

("OLD CLASSICS.")

Synopsis of Lecture by Mr. Fred. J. Melville at the Opening Meeting of the Aberdeen and North of Scotland Philatelic Society, October 13th, 1920.

PART I.

INTRODUCTORY.—The Fascination of Stamp-Collecting.—The Romance of an Old (Oppen) Album, 1864.—The "Peny Post," 1680.—Twopenny Post, 1801.—Mulready's Envelope, 1840.—The First Adhesive Postage Stamps.—1d. Black and 2d. Blue.—The 1d. "V.R."—The Penny Stamp goes Red!—1d. Red lettered "B" only.—Perforation Trials.—The Prince Consort Essay.—The 1½d. Error OP.PC.—The Small ½d. Stamp, 1870. Plate 9.—Embossed Stamps.—Dickinson Paper.—Oxford Union Society.—Oxford and Cambridge College Stamps.—High Values £1 and £5 (Queen)—Official Stamps.—Government Parcels, Inverted.—"I.R. Official."—£1 Queen and King Edward, in Blocks of Four.—The Stock Exchange Forgery.

PART II.

Switzerland: Zurich. Divisible Stamp of Geneva.—Brazil: "Bull's Eye."—United States Postmaster's Stamps. Confederate States.—Mauritius: "Post Office" and "Monkey's Head."—France; "Tete-beche."—British Guiana: "Circular." "Patimus." Type-set Stamps re-constructed (1862).—Saxony.—Prussia.—Spain.—New South Wales: Sydney Views and View of Sydney. Victoria Lithographs; Queen on Throne.—Nova Scotia. New Brunswick. Canada.—Hawaiian Missionaries.—Tuscany: 3-lire.—Holland.—India: 4-annas (Inverted Head).—Roman States: Reunion.—Three-cornered Capes.—Woodblocks.—Van Diemen's Land: 4d. 1853 in a strip. The London-printed Issue, 1855.—Western Australia: Inverted Swan.—Ceylon: 4d. Rose.—Corrientes.—Sweden: "tretio" for "tjugo".—Uruguay: The Missing Links.—Moldavia.—Naples "Cross."—Sicily: King Bomba.—Nevis.—St. Vincent 5s.—Egypt.—Heligoland.—Uganda.—Newfoundland.

The synopsis prepared for the public lecture by Melville in 1920.

Turtle" (potages) and "Rissoles of Worn Plates" (entrées)[8]. "Serbian Pudding" was presumably a reference to the interests of the visiting President

On 29 November 1922 another visit was made, this one more locally, to see the assembly of news and production of the last *Aberdeen Free Press*. In much later years, visits were made to the GPO. An unusual subject was scheduled for the meeting of 7 January 1925, when members competed in detecting forgeries!

By 1929 the balance of the annual programme had clearly shifted towards displays of the stamps of particular countries, with displays of Uruguay, USA (2), Crete and Siam, Argentina, China and Hong Kong, seven out of the eleven normal meetings. A continued feeling of responsibility to instruct is evident, however, in talks during the 1930-31 season on "Collecting, Exchanging, Buying and Selling" and on "What to Look For and What to Avoid in Collecting" by two senior members.

Throughout the 1930s, Junior Night, which had been a short-lived annual event in the early 1920s, was restored as a regular event. An airmail presentation also became frequent, whilst the range of countries appearing on the syllabus for the first time expanded considerably. Visiting speakers from a distance were becoming more frequent, with five such invitees in 1932. Also that same year the well-known professional philatelist, Robson Lowe, offered to address the Society on "This Business of Stamp Collecting" whilst visiting Scotland. The record of the meeting suggests that the speaker was combining business with pleasure, but he was to become a regular annual visiting speaker over the next five years and occasionally during the post-war period. He was evidently a popular speaker, because his advertised visit in 1936 necessitated the hire of a larger hall than the Society's usual venue in the Adelphi, well justified by

---

[8] "Dundee Dines with Aberdeen", *Stamp Collecting*, 7.4.23, 14.

an attendance of 118 members and friends. Typical of other invited speakers was James Durham, President of the Scottish PS, who was scheduled to display Newfoundland on 12 November 1931, but also presented an unannounced display of early USA. Visiting speakers apparently felt free to display fine material of their own choosing. In 1933 C.W. Meredith from Broughty Ferry visited the Society to display Colonial Airmails. He was accompanied by his wife who spoke unscheduled on the stamps of Palestine, Syria and the Lebanon from a biblical and historical point of view. She is recorded as the first lady to address the Society in its twenty-three years of existence and the Merediths became frequent visitors. Indeed, several visiting speakers became regular visitors to the Society in successive years in the 1930s, e.g., James Durham from Edinburgh, Dr A.E. Kidd from Dundee and A.B. Clements from Glasgow.

By the 1930s evening meetings were not exclusively devoted to philatelic topics. A display of the stamps of Soviet Russia on 6 November 1930 was followed by a talk by the President of the Aberdeen Chamber of commerce on "the economic, social and moral conditions obtaining under Soviet rule", which is said to have added greatly to the interest of the evening. Perhaps the most remarkable non-philatelic presentation was given on 22 February 1934 by Col. A.E. Stewart of Ballater who gave an address on his out-door hobby of tiger hunting!

The acquisition by the Society of its own premises in 1934 was coincident with a proposal that the Society should meet informally on alternate weeks between regular meetings. Only the dates of these meetings appeared in the syllabus, but a local speaker was invited to display at these meetings, except for a small number which were set aside for "exchange and gossip". The meetings continued throughout the three seasons that the Society retained its premises at the Adelphi, but only three were held in the following season, when they seem to have been largely incorporated and formalised within an extended programme for 1927-28. Thirty-three of these "Informal

Meetings" took place and it is perhaps a measure of the success of the Society at that time that weekly meetings could be sustained and that the meetings were mostly well supported. The meetings almost all took the form of collections on display, with several countries usually on show on any one night. By contrast, the greater formality of regular meetings is apparent in that speakers customarily "read a paper before and during the display", which may account for the popularity of informal nights.

At an informal meeting on 28 February 1935, there is evidence of interest in what was to become the recognised form of thematic philately. The display "was of a Zoological nature and departed from the usual routine of mounting, all stamps showing the same type of animal being together irrespective of the country to which they belonged". This was not, of course, the first display to the Society which can be categorised as thematic, but it is really not until 1931 that titles appear on the formal syllabus (The Story Of Columbus, Saints in Philately) that might be interpreted as thematic in today's terms.

An innovation in the programme came about on 25 November 1937, with an entire evening devoted a "Private Stamp Sale" by Margaret Davidson, a dealer in postage stamps from Glasgow who had displayed to the Society in the previous year. The event was not repeated, although she continued to advertise in the syllabus.

Weekly meetings were sustained for only the first half of the 1938-39 season, when three meetings were devoted to "practical demonstrations" on mounting collections, printing, perforations and papers, and identifying forgeries. Members were perhaps surprised to learn that "the earliest suggestion as to perforation of postage stamps came from an Aberdonian - Mr John Blaikie". With the outbreak of war in 1939, meetings were not resumed until the winter of 1941, when the last of the two meetings held that year included a display of Germany. The Society continued to meet sporadically into 1942, but a normal syllabus of meetings was resumed for 1942-43. The President's Night of that season saw the first showing by Dr V.M.M. Watson of what became a familiar collection within the Society, his "Compendium of Philatelic Terms illustrated with Actual Stamps and Descriptive Notes", in which he defined and illustrated on that occasion, for example, forty-one types of stamps for postal use, fifty-nine processes of stamp printing and thirty-six main types of papers. He presented "further additions" in the following season and in 1949 his compendium was described as a work of art in two volumes. The continuation of an educative flavour to the programme is also evident in the "Any Questions?" meeting of 19 November 1942, when a number of erudite, obscure and demanding questions were put to the panel of local experts.

The recognition within the hobby of what would now be seen as Cinderella subjects becomes apparent from the 1940s. For example, air mail etiquettes form part of the subject matter of an evening in 1943 and in 1945 an entire evening was devoted to charity seals and labels, whilst registration labels were exhibited on another occasion that year. There is also evidence in displays of the way in which collectors continued to assemble collections from a great range of countries. A display in 1945 included stamps from no less than thirty-five countries around the Pacific. Another evening in the same year entitled "Andorra, etc." was equally devoted to Eire and Spain. The inclusion of numbers of different countries in their own right, not necessarily in the context of a theme, within the displays by a single speaker continued as a regular practice into the 1950s. Diversity of collecting interests is noted in 1947 as a "tendency now-a-days to branch into side-lines".

Lantern slides had long been used occasionally in evening presentations and colour film strip was also utilised by 1949. The 1950-51 season saw the first evening consisting of a film display, on this occasion films loaned through the Swiss Tourist Office on stamp printing techniques. There were five other film nights between then and 1976.

From the 1950s the strict formality which was thought appropriate in the conduct of meetings was gradually relaxed. In 1952 it was formally proposed that on nights where a guest was speaking, the business part of the meeting should be delayed until his departure, a suggestion which met with approval, but which was viewed as not strictly constitutional. The stated policy of the committee in drawing up annual programmes was for displays to be "fairly light and varied". Philately remained, nevertheless, a serious subject. The AGM of 1952 unanimously approved a motion that "in view of the widely varying and diverse interests of its members, certain meetings or additional meetings should be in the form of study circles". The motion was referred to the Committee for implementation, but additional meetings seem not to have been scheduled and it is not clear whether there was any conscious attempt to implement the resolution.

In the 1950s thematic topics and members' thematic evenings became regular events. Thematic collecting in the Society in the 1950s and 1960s was encouraged by the several displays given by a visitor from Glasgow, Capt. Philippe Durand, who was a great enthusiast and advocate of that form of collecting[9]. At one meeting a mock coronation was held and he was given the title of "Thematicus Rex" in recognition of his contribution to the study of stamp design.

A notable visitor in 1954 was Kenneth F. Chapman, Editor of *Stamp Collecting*, who was presented with an inscribed cigarette case. He responded by saying that this was the first time that he had been so honoured. Another visitor of note, if only for the frequency of his visits, was the Glasgow stamp dealer, Alex McConnell, who

---

[9] Gardiner, Stewart, 2005, *The Caledonian Philatelic Society 1906-2006*, Caledonian Philatelic Society, Glasgow, 15-16.

displayed new issues of the world. The title of his presentation, "Round the World in 1959", changed each year for the next six years, only by bringing forward the date by one year. Each year he apparently brought members up to date with some 200 pages of new issues, on occasion making sales.

The syllabus for the 1959-60 season incorporated what appears to be an innovation in the form of "short talks of a tutorial nature following the meetings". Only two of these are recorded, on sheet margins and papers, and they do not appear in later years.

The 1963-64 season saw the first of what quickly became a regular feature of annual programmes, a display by four members of the Arbroath PS, the closest philatelic society to Aberdeen. The visit was reciprocated next season, when the visitors to Aberdeen, rather surprisingly, were from the Ayr PS. Since 1966 there have only been four seasons when representatives of a visiting Society were not welcomed, although on one occasion, the visitors went to the wrong venue and returned home in confusion! The Society has enjoyed regular exchange visits with the Arbroath, Moray and Dundee societies, and less frequently with Perth PS.

In 1967 a procedural change was introduced which has remained in place. It was decided that the customary practice of scheduling the President's Night on the first night of each new season should be changed. In future the opening night of the season was to be informal, without a full evening's display. The change proved to be immediately popular, with high attendances, and this situation has remained ever since. A number of minor events have taken place in the informal opening nights, including visits by dealers, demonstrations of philatelic techniques, silent displays and a quiz, but it has evolved primarily into a social evening of stamp trading and exchange between members.

Professional visitors from afar continued to provide occasional but characteristically well-attended displays, with P.A. Wilde in 1963, Robson Lowe in 1972, Francis Field in 1974 and 1975, Capt. K. Jahr in 1978 and 1991, Susan Worsley of Robson Lowe in 1979 and 1883, David Boyd of Philips in 1985 and 1989, Robert Murray in 1985 and 1993, Raif Wellsted in 1985, G.A. Childs of Harmers in 1989, J.L. Grimwood-Taylor of Cavendish in 1996, Alan Wishart in 2000 and 2006, Stewart Henderson of Phillips in 2007 and Michael Thompson of Bonhams in 2008.

Aberdeen's location has meant that it has always tended to rely primarily on local speakers to make up its programme. Despite the surprising readiness of visitors to travel long distances to give displays to the Aberdeen PS, not just in recent years, distance and cost has influenced the number of invited speakers over the years. A locally-based philatelist with a good collection is likely to be invited back at regular intervals. Particularly in the early years, the same names appear frequently, providing talks and displays on a range of different topics and countries. Among the polymaths of the past are George Milne, W. Edmund Bell, John Anderson, William Marshall, Col. A.E. Stewart, Dr V.M.M Watson and Cdr. M.S.L. Burnett. Moreover, the frequent appearance of some countries in the syllabus can sometimes be associated with individual members of the Society, e.g. Canada, Hawaii, Switzerland, Zanzibar and India.

Over the entire history of the Society, no less than 130 stamp issuing countries are named in annual programmes. Not surprisingly, Great Britain in one form or another, including Scottish postal history, appears on fifty-six occasions, by far the largest, followed by Canada (25); Germany (15), India and USA (14 each); Australia (11), France (10); Hong Kong, New Zealand and Switzerland (8); China, Egypt, Jamaica (7); Falklands, Malta and West Indies (6); Austria, Holland, Norway, Poland, Denmark and South Africa (5). A further fifty-five countries are named on two to four occasions, whilst fifty-three countries appear only once. These figures are only indicative. They are not accurate tallies of the total number of occasions that the stamps of specific countries have actually been presented to members, since speakers did not confine themselves to a title and some titles are not country-specific. Nor do the figures include Presidential addresses, where the subject matter is not declared before the event. They certainly demonstrate the catholic tastes of the membership.

Another way in which past programmes demonstrate the locational factor of Aberdeen in the compilation of annual programmes of meetings is the use of local talent and enthusiasm in what might be loosely termed members' nights, when several or many speakers each made a small contribution. Usually some sort of theme is adopted for the evening and these have taken a great many ingenious forms, dating back to 1911. Since then members have been invited or cajoled to contribute to My Favourite Country, Ladies Night, King George V, War Stamps, Question Night, Ten Minute Papers, Single Sheet Display, Debate, The World's Most Handsome Stamp, Bring Along Your Stamps, Airmail Night, Quiz Night, Sponsored Night, Six Interesting Sheets, Six Sheets of Covers, Past-Presidents' Night, The Committee Entertains, Six Sheets of Foreign Stamps, New Members Display, Koffee Koolers' Night, Six Sheets of Thematics, Sea and Rail Postmarks, Europe, Africa, The Americas, Asia, Gibbons Pt 1, Gibbons Pt 2, Gibbons Pt 3, Cinderellas, My Latest Acquisitions, Latin America, GLASGOW 2000 revisited, Autobiography Night, The Spirit of Philately, Your Number is Up, A Few of My Favourite Things, Colour Me Red, Something from My Collection and Anything Goes! One further form of a participatory night commenced for the first time in 1985, when the letter for Alphabet Night was the letter A. Since then alphabet night has been an annual event, usually on the first meeting of the New Year and included in the programme with remorseless logic, so that Z is due in 2011.

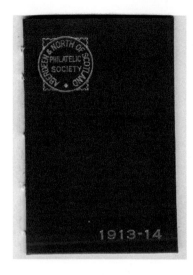

ABERDEEN PHILATELIC SOCIETY

Founded 1910
for the study of all branches of Philately

The Society meets in
Rubislaw Church Centre,
Fountainhall Road,
Queens Cross, Aberdeen
at 7.30 p.m.
on the dates given

2002 - 2003

The syllabus for 1913-14 and for 2002-03

Visits from other Societies have been a regular feature of the programme since the 1960s, reflecting increased mobility. A visitor from Moray PS puts up his display of Malta.

Chapter 4

A Fluctuating Membership

At the start of the first season in 1910, the Society had already enrolled twenty-seven members and by the end of that season the membership had increased to forty-nine. In the following three seasons prior to the Great War, numbers gradually rose to sixty-six. During the war membership records were effectively frozen. The Society became fully operational again in the 1919-20 season with a senior membership[10] of about sixty.

Membership rose consistently throughout the 1920s to 139 in 1931, before holding steady during the economic difficulties of the early 1930s. In the latter half of that decade numbers started to rise again to 163 at the outbreak of the second world war. Membership records were again frozen during the early years of the war and with resumption of a full range of activities in 1942, numbers remained at a similar level until immediately after the war, when they took off. By 1947 they had reached 194 and in 1951 they reached the highest-ever total of 310, reflecting a time of very wide interest in philately. It is difficult to envisage a society of so many active members. A significant proportion of the membership might have joined to access the exchange packet.

The high figure was not sustained, however. Indeed, numbers slowly declined to 209 in 1956 and settled around this figure for a few years. In the first half of the 1960s the decline continued to 150 and remained around or slightly above that figure until 1981. In the 1980s membership was closer to 110, before declining again in 1990 to eighty. The 1990s saw a further slow decline to between sixty-five and seventy. Membership numbers have stabilised at that level in recent years.

---

[10] The more volatile Junior membership numbers are discussed in chapter 7.

Aberdeen Philatelic Society 1910-2010

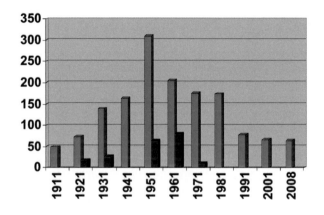

Membership numbers

Chapter 5

The Conduct of Meetings: More or Less Formal

The records suggest that during the few years of the Society's existence before the first world war, the content of meetings and the manner in which they were conducted were not to a set pattern. Different formats were experimented with. The very first meeting took the form of a lecture ("President's Address on Philately"). The second meeting was also "a lecture", albeit illustrated with exhibits, supplied in part by other members. Five of the eleven meetings in that first session were entitled "Display: ..." setting them apart as a different form of meeting compared to the other six. "Papers" were regularly read. For example, a paper on India was described as being more interesting because it was accompanied by the speaker's collection of India, as if the paper was the main event and the stamps mere illustration.

There is a different flavour to programmes as from the second season, with evenings designed to allow the participation of several members, for example, five-minute papers. On other occasions several members showed stamps or contributed displays on the subject of the evening in support of the main speaker, who was not always present in person, but sent his pages and accompanying notes to the Society. In the abridged 1915-16 season, all meetings included "Displays by Members", an arrangement presumably arising from the uncertainties of wartime. Lantern slides were in use by 1912. Formal discussion of matters of interest are recorded, for example, concern that over 1,000 stamps had been issued in 1912.

Papers evidently continued to be serious presentations. A paper on stamp printing processes delivered at the second meeting of the Society in 1910 was the first of several by George Milne on the technicalities of philately which were subsequently published in *The Stamp Collector's Fortnightly*.

With the post-war resumption of a normal syllabus in 1919, participation by members at every meeting was actively sought. To quote the 1919-20 syllabus: "Members are requested to contribute to the Displays at all meetings, whether collections be mounted on loose leaves or bound albums." This was, of course, a time when it was still common to collect generally, across a wide range of countries. The arrangement was, no doubt, appropriate to a time when the Society was seeking to rekindle participation and enthusiasm for the hobby, and to increase membership. It was in that same context, that the committee debated who of the following: Fred J. Melville, J.E. Heginbottom and Percy C. Bishop, be invited, in co-operation with the Societies in Edinburgh, Glasgow and Dundee, to lecture on the opening night of the 1920-21 season.

Meetings were conducted formally, from the Chair. Minutes were read and after approval they were signed by the Chairman. Applications for membership were proposed, seconded and formally put to the meeting. Other business was conducted similarly from the Chair. The same formality evidently extended to committee meetings which occasionally became very argumentative, with formal motions voted on and sometimes vigorously contested.

Exactly how stamps were actually displayed to members attending meetings at that time is not certain. The report in the *Aberdeen Daily Journal* of an address to the Society on 21 February 1921 by John Anderson states that his address "was copiously illustrated on the blackboard and by means of stamps...". The venue for the meeting was a school classroom, which explains the blackboard, but it is not clear whether album pages were laid out on tables or passed from hand to hand, with or without protection. One visiting speaker in 1923, whose talk to the Society was very fully recorded in the philatelic press,[11] said that "he was not a believer in too many

---

[11] "Fifty Years as a Philatelist. Dr F. Collie Delights Aberdeen Stamp Collectors", *Stamp Collecting*, 7 April 1923, 7.

displays...that he had some specimens to show, but they were ... only of interest because of their personal appeal to himself." He apparently regaled his audience with a fund of stories, rather than showing many stamps. Among the suggestions at the AGM in 1923 it was formally proposed that there should be a "display of stamps at each meeting", but no mention of the manner in which stamps should be displayed. Perhaps this implies that there was an accepted practice when stamps were displayed. The President's address at the start of the following season was illustrated with lantern slides, but on a couple of occasions later that season sheets were "passed round" or "handed round". It is not clear whether some form of protection was provided. Ten years on we read of Edmund Bell's collection of Colonials being passed round for inspection. In 1939 the committee considered acquiring trestles to show sheets of exhibits, but nothing came of it.

Contemporary social attitudes are reflected at the meeting of 23 January 1936, when the President, presiding over a large attendance, "made graceful reference to the death of our late monarch King George". Were philatelists, whose hobby brought them into frequent contact with the image of the monarch, himself a notable philatelist, particularly affected? Only three months previously, when the Society had celebrated its Silver Jubilee, a telegram of loyal greetings had been sent to the King (in his Silver Jubilee year). In response, the Society had received a telegram from Sandringham. Perhaps another reflection of contemporary society is that in January 1939, in proposing a vote of thanks to the participants of "Ladies Night", the evening was described as "a real revelation to many"!

Telegram from a Private Secretary, Sandringham, in 1935, the silver jubilee year of both the Society and HM King George V, thanking the Society for "their kind and loyal greetings".

With the resumption of normal activities after the war, meetings continued to be conducted with due formality, if not solemnity. At the start of each meeting, the minutes of the last meeting were duly read and approved. Evidently, they were listened to with care and attention, as amendments were occasionally entered. One has the impression that the more senior members of long-standing ensured that proper procedures were duly followed. Their role was to guide and encourage in what they saw as best practice, not only informally, but on occasion, through programmed talks. George Milne, who was Curator of the Forgeries Collection and Convener of the Expert Committee for more than forty years, delivered his talk on "Four Aspects of Philately" (collecting, exchanging, buying and selling) on four occasions. He counselled, for example, against buying stamps in postal auctions where prospective purchases could not be examined at first hand. Formal motions might be put to any meeting, not just to the AGM. In October 1945, what seems to have been a vigorous debate on a motion to approach the Postmaster General on the subject of a Victory issue, was caught up in procedural matters before being carried. Formality in the conduct of meetings did not, however, prevent controversy. In that same year, the presenter of a display of commemoratives of the USSR was questioned from the floor on their legitimacy!

A proposal which was perhaps indicative of the status of the Society in the minds of the membership, was made at the conclusion of the meeting in 1951. It was agreed that "a telegram be sent to Her Majesty the Queen on 5 October ... Aberdeen Philatelic Society with humble duty tenders sincerest good wishes for His Majesty's continued restoration to health." A telegram was received in response on 14 October.

From the 1950s the strict formality which had been thought appropriate in the conduct of meetings was gradually relaxed. In 1952 it was formally proposed that on nights when a guest was speaking, the business part of the meeting should be delayed until his departure, a suggestion which met with approval, but which was viewed as not strictly constitutional. The reason, in part, may have been that, at that time, it was normal practice for the Chairman to invite members to raise questions and comments towards the end of meetings, when the Chairman presided over a period of formal discussion. Displays from visitors often prompted much discussion and hence more time was needed.

Not all meetings were solemn occasions. At a meeting in 1952, addressed by E.W.S. Jupp, "members were holding their sides with laughter". Non-philatelic displays supplementing short philatelic displays, were occasionally acceptable, e.g. slides of Malaya by the former Post Master General of Malaya in 1955, on Antarctica in 1959 and on St Kilda in 1992. In 1954 a scheduled talk on "Trees and

Flowers on Stamps" was replaced at short notice by an illustrated talk on "African Witch Doctors"!

Stamps on display continued to be passed around in the 1950s, although there was an attempt at a radical change in viewing procedures in 1949, when the venue for meetings changed from the Oddfellows' Rooms to the Round Room of the Music Hall. The committee decided to experiment with the use of frames owned by the Society for use at exhibitions. They agreed to try to use frames arranged around the room for the President's night, the opening night of the 1949-50 season, but lack of storage facilities at the Music Hall and costs of cartage defeated the attempt. At that time, what were described as "acetate display folders", were used when handing sheets around, and the Society acquired a smart wooden case to contain them, made and donated by Ian Smillie, an item still in the Society's possession. It facilitated the transport of the folders and their contents to and from the home of any member displaying to the Society.

In 1959 A.S. Mackie and Dr V.M.M. Watson constructed two double-sided display racks which they donated to the Society. By then the Society had moved to the YMCA, but it appears that the use of the new display boards was spasmodic, with sheets still being passed around at some, if not most meetings. In 1963 a visiting professional philatelist, P.A. Wilde of Cardiff, was pointedly recorded as using the display boards, but two years later a member complained of the rather dilapidated state of the folders, which must therefore have remained in frequent use. For a few years thereafter display boards were used occasionally, for example at the opening and informal night of the season, when a silent display was appropriate. At normal meetings sheets continued to be passed round in folders. New transparent folders were acquired in 1975, each with a numbered backing sheet and an image of the Adelphi Post Office in 1840.

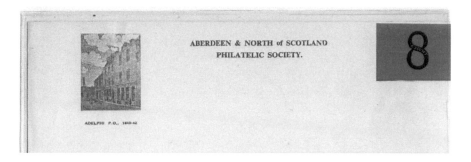

ABERDEEN & NORTH of SCOTLAND
PHILATELIC SOCIETY.

8

ADELPHI P.O., 1840-42

The upper part of the transparent folders and backing sheets brought
in to use in 1975, for the circulation of displays at meetings

In 1977 the committee was asked to consider the use of display
boards and the members were said to be in favour, but the then
current venue was not well suited. With more than forty members
present in quite a small room in the YWCA, the boards caused
congestion at the opening meeting, although they were used on
another occasion that same season.

The use and the storage of the display boards were in part the reason
for the move to a new venue in 1978. The large and well-lighted
upper room in Northern Arts Club allowed display boards to come
into regular use. The two double-sided display boards were
converted into four single-sided free-standing boards by a member,
Charles Keith, a joiner by profession. They could now be arranged
around the room against the wall, although their use was not to
everyone's liking. In 1984 their use was debated but there was little
support for a return to passing pages from hand to hand, although
there arc, of course, societies in Scotland where that practice
continues. The same display boards continue to serve the Society
well to this day.

Attendance at meetings is presumably influenced by both the
attractiveness of the venue and the atmosphere in which meetings are
conducted and has quite frequently been a matter for concern. In its

very first season between ten and twenty-four members attended each meeting, the lowest number for the AGM, not surprisingly! Attendances remained of that order prior up to the Great War, and whilst there are no exact figures for attendance through the 1920s and 1930s, there are frequent references to large attendances, probably of the order of fifty or sixty. There were also meetings when the attendance was "most disappointing" or "smaller than usual, [due to] inclement weather", at a time of wider use of public transport. The first meeting of the 1937-38 season saw a record attendance of over seventy members, a figure substantially exceeded by an attendance of 110 in 1946 and by the all-time record of 112 in 1947-48, when the average attendance was seventy-eight. The post-war years saw the highest attendance figures in the history of the Society. By the 1950s they were falling off to the forties and fifties and by the 1950s to the thirties. By 1966 "grave concern" was expressed, as attendances fell as low as twenty, but the tendency into the 1970s was upward again towards thirty and beyond in the 1980s. Average attendances have remained in the thirties ever since. It is interesting that Aberdeen PS seems to have countered what is often said to be the current trend of declining attendances at Society meetings and has stabilised since its low point in the 1960s.

A relatively recent innovation has taken the form of very informal fortnightly morning meetings. A proposal to hold such meetings was aired at the start of the 1998-99 season and quickly implemented on 11 November at Rubislaw Church Centre. Since then ten or fifteen members have met for coffee and conversation. Minimal organisation is required for Friday morning meetings of an essentially social nature, when a few stamps may change hands. These meetings no doubt reflect the rising age-profile of the membership.

Chapter 6

Exhibiting at Home and Away

One of the ways in which the Society has changed over the years is in its propensity to arrange public exhibitions of stamps. The membership of recent years would probably be surprised to learn of the frequency of exhibitions in Aberdeen in the early years when staging such events was evidently seen as an important function of the Society.

From its outset the Society was financially supportive of the Philatelic Congress of Great Britain, particularly in 1913, when it was held in Edinburgh, when members were invited to exhibit and delegates appointed to attend. Soon after the end on the first world war, however, the Society began to organise local exhibitions on its own initiative. At a committee meeting on 1st October 1919, it was agreed to hold an exhibition of war stamps, to stimulate interest in philately and with a view to increasing membership. The exhibition was held in the YMCA at what seems like extraordinarily short notice, thirty days later. It was open for two hours on one evening, but it was very much a public event, advertised in the *Aberdeen Free Press* and the *Aberdeen Daily Journal*, with a charge for admission.

AN EXHIBITION OF WAR STAMPS,
By Members of the
ABERDEEN PHILATELIC SOCIETY.
Will be held in the Y.M.C.A., 198 Union Street,
On FRIDAY, 31st inst., from 8-10 p.m.
Tickets 6d (including tax) at the door, or
from the Secretary.
W. EDMUND BELL,
35a Union Street, Aberdeen.

Advertisement for an exhibition of war stamps,
Aberdeen Free Press 31.10.19.

35

The exhibition is on record as "a fine display of the issues brought about by the war", and it was also the first meeting of the Society for the 1919-20 season. It was well attended and the membership was apparently considerable augmented. In consequence, another evening exhibition was arranged in the following season, a much grander affair held in the Ball Room of the Music Hall on 8 December, 1920.

There is a fuller record of the 1920 exhibition. A provisional committee was set up to organise the event and members were invited to contribute. The committee selected 160 sheets of stamps and nine cards of war entires lent by nineteen members. In addition, cards with stamps of particular interest to juniors and loaned by Fred J. Melville were on show, as well as Stanley Gibbons' exhibition series no. 2, arranged to interest juniors in the hobby. The committee rejected the idea of placing exhibits under glass as too expensive. Sheets were mounted on cards with a gelatine protecting cover over each sheet and the cards were placed on forms arranged around the hall. The exhibits were insured against fire and burglary for £1000. Tickets for the event were printed and distributed to members for sale, with the price of admission at 9d for adults and 6d for juniors (including tax of 3d and 1d!). The event was again advertised in the press.

A report on the exhibition in the *Evening Express* described it as "undoubtedly the most representative ever held by the society" and mentioned that it attracted hundreds of collectors and others, despite the fact that it was only open on one evening from 7.30 to 10pm. The display included early British Guiana, 54 Cape triangulars, 63 pence Ceylon, 55 penny blacks, 22 twopenny blues, two Sydney views, Mulready caricatures, a specialised collection of Belgian Congo and early USA with essays and proofs. Ticket receipts of £11.4.6 suggest an attendance of some 400, whilst the exhibition account showed a credit balance of £1.1.7.

In the 1921-22 season it was decided that one of the regular meetings would again take the form of a public exhibition and the Ball Room of the Music Hall was booked for 1 March 1922. On this occasion 500 adult and 500 junior tickets were printed, price 9d and 4d. Five junior members exhibited for the first time, as well as eighteen senior members. In total, 124 sheets were on display with 1870 stamps, six entires and nine postcards, the junior contribution amounting to fourteen of the sheets with 155 stamps. The tally emphasises the way in which the hobby was predominantly concerned with stamps. Postal history was still in the future.

A report on the exhibition in the *Daily Free Press* was headlined "STAMP EXHIBITION. Unique specimens shown in Aberdeen". Items singled out for special mention included "the earliest issues from Bagdad", specimens from German East Africa used in the colony during the war and "printed on paper made from rice", and "a South of Ireland provisional".

The following year the junior members borrowed the Society's cardboard and gelatine covers to mount a public exhibition in the Parlour of the YMCA on 7 February 1923, opened by the President and in aid of Gordons College Recreation Ground. Fifteen junior members exhibited and were complimented on a very fine display. A prize was donated for the best single-sheet display of used stamps.

The next "Grand Exhibition" to be staged as a part of the annual programme of meetings was on 17 November 1926, again in the Ball Room of the Music Hall. The arrangements and publicity were very much as before, but with a limit of 120 exhibits and the adult admission down to 6d. It appears that these events were becoming almost routine, with the Exhibition Committee only convening to decide on the arrangements two weeks before the event. In any event, the exhibition "was well attended and cleared all expenses".

ABERDEEN AND NORTH OF SCOTLAND PHILATELIO SOCIETY.

EXHIBITION OF POSTAGE STAMPS
In BALL ROOM, MUSIC HALL BUILDINGS,
On WEDNESDAY, 17th November, 1926,
7.30 p.m. to 9.30 p.m.
Admission 6d; Juniors 4d.
W. A. FLEMING, Hon. Sec.
58 Forest Avenue, Aberdeen.

Advertisement in the *Evening Express* for the exhibition of 1926.

A two-day exhibition proposed for 1928 did not materialise, but the 1930-31 season saw another public exhibition as part of the syllabus in December 1930. Once again it took place in the Ball Room of the Music Hall and was described as "most successful". The Treasurer in reporting a deficit stated that the benefit in publicity and membership far outweighed the financial loss. The exhibition gave rise to what must be one of the rarities of philatelic literature. A thirteen-page *Report of Exhibition* was published privately by W. Edmund Bell in a numbered edition of seventy-five copies, a pamphlet on glossy paper consisting mainly of reprints of the accounts published in the *Aberdeen Press and Journal* for 5 and 6 December, 1930.

The year 1931 was the twenty-first anniversary of the founding of the Society and an exhibition was proposed as an afternoon and evening event on 10 October, the date when the first meeting was held. The usual venue was unfortunately not available on that date and the event was scheduled for 22 October, from 7 to 9.30pm. In preparation for this exhibition, the Society acquired fifty oak frames fitted with glass, three-ply backs and cards, suitable for taking four sheets of stamps. Two hundred sheets were consequently on display in the new frames at what was described as a highly successful exhibition with a large attendance of members and the general public. It proved to be the last of the public exhibitions held on one evening as part of the annual programme of Society meetings.

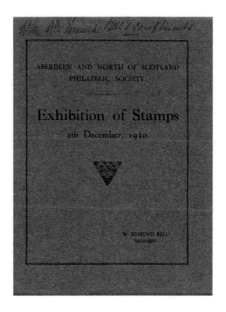

ABERDEEN AND NORTH OF SCOTLAND
PHILATELIC SOCIETY.

—·:·—

REPORT OF EXHIBITION

HELD IN THE

BALL-ROOM, MUSIC HALL,
ABERDEEN,

On THURSDAY, 4th December, 1930,

Together with Illustrated Article which appeared in the
"Aberdeen Press and Journal"

On SATURDAY, 6th December, 1930.

W. EDMUND BELL, 352 Union Street, Aberdeen.

Privately printed January, 1931.

Report of the 1930 exhibition. Seventy-five copies
were privately printed, of which this is No. 44.

In January 1932 the Society signed a formal agreement with the Public Library Committee in Aberdeen to allow for a permanent display of stamps in the Central Library, the sheets in the display case to be changed from time to time by the Society. A similar agreement was entered into for a permanent display using frames in the Art Gallery. The furniture was commissioned and then installed in both venues by March 1932 and brought into use at once by the newly appointed Superintendent of the Permanent Exhibitions. Members were requested to submit sheets of stamps for display.

The negotiations with City officials to install permanent exhibitions in two venues gave rise to a much larger event. During the course of those negotiations the Curator of the Art Gallery offered to put a room in the Gallery at the disposal of the Society for a month-long exhibition. This is perhaps an indication of contemporary attitudes towards the hobby, confirmed by the positive response from the Director of Education when asked to facilitate the distribution of publicity in Secondary Schools.

In preparation for the exhibition ten more frames were ordered, members were invited to submit suitable sheets of stamps, fire insurance of £1000 was taken out and exhibitors were asked to contribute one shilling towards the cost of insurance. The Committee decided to approach Sir Thomas Jaffray, Chairman of the Art Gallery Committee to perform the opening ceremony, "whom failing Mr J.G. Burnett of Powis, M.P. for North Aberdeen". The order of precedence is interesting! In any event, it was the Member of Parliament who duly performed the opening ceremony on the evening of Saturday 3 December. In his address he referred to the Free Letters to which, in former days, Members of Parliament were entitled. The ceremony was advertised in the *Evening Express* as "All interested cordially invited. Admission FREE" (never fails in Aberdeen!), 250 invitation cards were printed for circulation and there was much debate about the provision of tea and at whose expense.

A catalogue was printed, price one penny, listing the contents of the sixty frames and indicative of the contemporary predominance of collecting stamps by countries, with only occasional mention of postmarks, covers, airmails, postal history or stamps by theme, one exception being "Last St Kilda mails". The event was described as an unqualified success, with an estimated attendance of some 250 persons daily. The Curator of the Art Gallery must have been pleased with attendance because he let it be known that should the Society wish to hold another exhibition, he could offer a larger room and fifteen additional small frames. The continuing success of the permanent exhibitions through the 1930s may have mitigated against acceptance of the offer. There were occasional difficulties in organising fresh material for those displays, which suggests that finding new material for another very much larger exhibition might not have been easy.

Preparations for an exhibition commenced in April 1939, but were overtaken by the outbreak of hostilities. Then in 1940 an exhibition in aid of the Red Cross was proposed, but it seems not to have taken place. In 1943 the Society was approached by the War Comforts Co-ordination Committee to support a fair in the Music Hall with a sale of stamps and an exhibition. The Society agreed in principle to participate, but eventually withdrew on the grounds of inadequate space and facilities. Having committed itself to support the charity in principle, the Society set about organising an exhibition in the Art Gallery with a collection box in the entrance in support of a Prisoners of War Fund. Similar arrangements to the 1932 exhibition were made and the exhibition took place from 15 to 31 October 1943. Attendance was "satisfactory", the sum of £9 was collected and this was increased to £10 from Society funds and donated to the POW charity. At about the same time the permanent exhibitions, which had gone into abeyance because of the war, were restarted.

ABERDEEN AND NORTH OF SCOTLAND
PHILATELIC SOCIETY.

EXHIBITION OF STAMPS,
- IN -
Art Gallery,
DECEMBER 3RD, 1932, TO JANUARY 3RD, 1933.

CATALOGUE. - ONE PENNY.

No.

1. Showing 2 Mulready Envelopes, Portrait of Inventor of Stamps, and P.O. Circular issued with start of Penny Postage, 1840.

2-5. Forgeries.

6 8. Great Britain, line engraved.

9. Commemorative Stamps—various countries.

10. Air Mail, flown covers.

11. French Colonies.

12. Belgium, including Congo and Danzig.

13-15 French Territory and Colonies.

16. Nyassa, Obock, Russia, Lithuania.

17. Spain and Dependency.

18. Great Britain and North Borneo.

19-26. Specialised collection of Cape of Good Hope with postal history

27. Newfoundland and Zanzibar.

The catalogue of the 1932-33 exhibition was a modest two-page list of exhibits.

The Exhibitions Committee reconvened in July 1944 to consider a second charitable exhibition, this time in aid of the Red Cross. The usual well-tried arrangements for publicity, insurance, selecting exhibits, mounting the displays, etc., were put in place and the event took place in the Art Gallery from 30 September to 15 October. This exhibition was novel in respect of content and arrangement. It was divided into the following sections, including a rather surprising last section: 1) Great Britain 1840 to present day - arranged in the form of a Pageant and including a small section on meter marks; 2) Queen Victoria British Colonials; 3) Edwardian British Colonials; 4) George V, Edward VIII and George VI British Colonials; 5) British Protectorates; 6) A foreign section; 7) an airmail section; 8) Red Cross, tuberculosis and health stamps; 9) war issues; 10) forgeries; 11) Nazi history - with comments. Quite what the thinking was behind this arrangement is not known. In any event, the exhibition resulted in a donation of £15.15 to the Red Cross.

The minutes of the AGM of 1 April 1948 briefly mention a proposed exhibition. The record of what appears to have been an unusually substantial event is strangely sparse, but there is a hint of unforeseen difficulties and frustration, perhaps because this was a larger event than had previously been staged and because of insufficient time allowed for its organisation. It took place in the Music Hall from 15 to 21 September 1948 and was open daily from 2 to 10pm. A measure of the strength of the hobby at that time is evident in that 2,500 people paid for admission (adults 6d, children 3d) and seventy-four new members were recruited, including thirty-three juniors. A Visitors' Book is in archives, but curiously contains only forty-three entries. A neat 20-page glossy illustrated souvenir Stamp Exhibition brochure was published containing six short articles by members, but with no mention of what was on display, apart from a short list of acknowledgements of "outstanding exhibits" which included Francis Field, Stanley Godden, Col. H.W. Hill of Oban, L.T. Vowles of Westbury-on-Severn, and the Commonwealth of Australia and the Dominion of New Zealand. The net was clearly cast widely in search of exhibitors for this event. It also included (without acknowledgement in the brochure) Capt. Philippe Durand of Glasgow who was renowned for his thematic displays. Frames for the event were seemingly hired at considerable cost. Three evening lectures were delivered during the exhibition and a long article on the educational value of stamp collecting by Dr V.M.M. Watson, a prominent member of the Society, appeared in *The Press and Journal* on 14 September. An exhibition label and a souvenir "Posted at the Exhibition" cover were produced. Despite problems which may have arisen in mounting what must have been the largest exhibition so far, in 1949 the Society proposed to organise another such event in the following year.

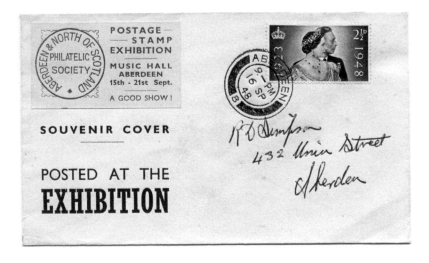

Souvenir cover commemorating the 1948 exhibition.

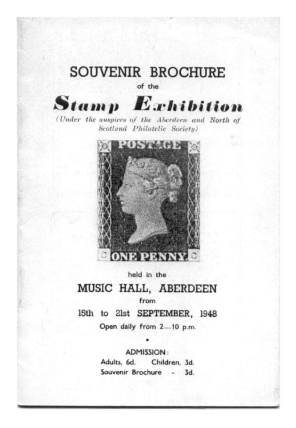

The 1948 exhibition brochure.

The 1950 exhibition was given the title of ANSPEX and was held in the Music Hall from 8 to 16 September. It is particularly remembered for a substantial associated publication, a 64-page Handbook with nine articles on philatelic topics including "A Short Postal History of Aberdeen". The handbook was priced at 1/6d in a card binding or 3/6d hard bound with gilt lettering. A review in Gibbons' Stamp Monthly described it as "quite the best "local" philatelic publication we have seen". Numbers sold are not recorded but a loss of some £20 on the Handbook account resulted in a deficit on the exhibition account of £7. Again, the admission charge (adults 6d, children 3d) was the main source of revenue, with numbers attending similar to 1948. Dealers' table rentals were not as significant a source of income as they tend to be more recently. Ten thousand "stickers" were also printed for the event. These were small publicity labels printed on gummed paper in a range of colours, showing the towers of Marischal and Kings College and designed for use on mail.

The 1950 exhibition was opened by Robson Lowe on the evening of 8 September and a report in the *Evening Express* describes some of the finer items on display. Reporting for a wider audience, it is the high values which are newsworthy. The headline reads "Farouk Stamps Caused a Furore", a reference to the story behind a unique block of four Egyptian Farouk wedding £1 stamps. Other major items were the GB Silver Jubilee 2_d Prussian blue error, classic USA, early Aden, rare first flights and early Aberdeen postal history. Sixty members contributed to a substantial display and the exhibition was again seen as a success "drawing many visitors from far off places: some visiting Aberdeen for the first time".

Some of the publicity labels produced for 1950 ANSPEX exhibition.

ANSPEX 1950: R.M. Hislop, philatelic auctioneer from Linlithgow, examines A.S. Mackie's exhibit of Zanzibar.

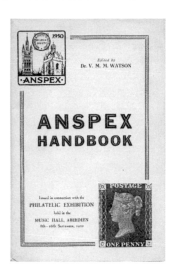

The ANSPEX Handbook, 1950

A signed copy of the centre pages of the 1950 ANSPEX Handbook.

In 1953 the Association of Scottish Philatelic Societies held its annual Congress in Aberdeen for the first and only time, and a public exhibition was organised by the host Society in the Music Hall from 4 to 11 April. It was advertised in the local press as "a super show"! It was opened by Charles Carter, Director of Aberdeen Art Gallery and a feature of the exhibition was the participation of *The Press and Journal*. The paper displayed a Volume de Luxe of *The Royal Philatelic Collection* by Sir John Wilson, together with a photographic display of the book's production. A second copy was also on display, presumably not the goatskin-bound de luxe edition. The C.W. Hornal collection of Aden once again attracted comment, as did displays of India and Scottish postmarks. The emergence of collecting by themes rather than country was exemplified by the Durand collection "which traced the descendants of Queen Victoria to thrones throughout Europe". The same report continued that the "exhibition was a triumph for Aberdeen Philatelists". Admission prices had doubled (adults 1/-, children 6d) and it was certainly a financial success with some £30 accruing to Society funds.

Another exhibition specifically designed to attract the public was held in the Music Hall from 3 to 8 September 1956 from 10am to 10pm, again under the title of ANSPEX and with the price of admission as in 1953. Curiously, it was described in the syllabus as the Society's third exhibition. Forty new frames were acquired and old ones refurbished for this event, which partly accounted for a financial deficit, but unfortunately it was not well supported. It was certainly well advertised by the Society in the local press, supported by adverts on successive days placed by a well known dealer at that time, R.M. Hislop of Linlithgow. A report headed "£10,000 worth on display in stamp show" in the *Press and Journal* described some of the exhibits, including proofs and colour trials from the Edward VII issue, Sperati forgeries and early Aberdeen postmarks. It was not a success in recruiting new senior members but interestingly "it proved of great value in the recruitment of juniors", evidence of the continued strength of the hobby amongst young people at that time. Indeed, there is incidental evidence of contemporary popular interest in stamp collecting in the *Evening Express* which ran two reports of philatelic matters unconnected to the exhibition during the week of the exhibition.

Nothing daunted, in 1957 the Society decided to celebrate its Golden Jubilee forthcoming in 1960 by holding "an exhibition finishing with a celebration dinner" and a Jubilee Fund was opened to defray the cost. The exhibition was held once again in the Music Hall from 28 March to 2 April from 2 to 10pm. Some seventy exhibits were reported to be on show, the main display being of stamps issued in 1910, when the Society was founded. A reporter for the *Press and Journal* recorded his meeting with an eighty-three year old member, the much respected John Fraser, whom he described as "a walking treasury of philatelic anecdotes...as they chatted, the youngsters were buzzing around like busy bees". The first visitors to the exhibition had, in fact, been thirty-five children from Mile End School Stamp Club, who had been "saving their pennies for three months to buy from the dealers". Attendance was regarded as "quite good" with about 1,114 visitors to the exhibition, but interest was clearly less than in some previous post-war events. The Presidents of all the Scottish philatelic societies were among the guests invited to the dinner and seven accepted. The guests included the Lord Provost of Aberdeen, George Stephen, who replied to the toast to 'non-philatelic' guests.

Golden Jubilee guest invitation.

An exhibition to celebrate the diamond jubilee of the Society in 1970 was fully discussed by the Committee in 1969, and it was decided not to proceed. A member approached the Public Library, nevertheless, where space was offered. The proposal was put to a full meeting of the Society, which reversed the Committee's decision and an exhibition was arranged in the Art Gallery from 4 July to 1 August. The sheets on display were changed weekly, so that some 500 sheets were displayed over the four week period, a major logistical exercise as one member of long standing emphatically recalls. Advertising for this exhibition was by means of posters distributed to schools, shops and sub-post offices. Admission was free and attendance consequently unknown, but at least twenty new members resulted.

Members of the Society have occasionally assisted in organising, or provided displays for visiting firms and auction houses, for example in 1971, in connection with the sale of the Cecil W. Meredith collection of Scots Local Cancellations by Robson Lowe which was available for viewing in the Station Hotel, Aberdeen.

The permanent exhibitions continued through the post-war period almost without a break until 1973, when the frames in the Art Gallery were removed. The display cases in the Central Library remained in use until 1982, when refurbishment necessitated their removal. At that point the long standing permanent exhibitions came to an end.

Thereafter storage of the Society's exhibition frames and cases was increasingly a problem and they were gradually disposed of. The last public exhibition in Aberdeen was in 1985, during the Society's seventy-fifth anniversary year. It was held on 4-25 May in the Art Gallery in rather cramped conditions with a display of 140 sheets in the Gallery's frames.

A request was made in 1989 to the City Arts Department for an exhibition in James Dun's House to commemorate the 150th anniversary of the first postage stamp, but it could not be accommodated. Although public exhibitions are so prominent in the history of the Society, they have not taken place over the past two decades. Their demise is, perhaps, indicative of the way in which both the hobby and the Society have evolved in recent years. Whilst the Society continues to contribute to philatelic exhibitions, it no longer seeks to reach a wider audience by staging public exhibitions, as it did so successfully when the mass appeal of the hobby was greater.

An exhibition in Aberdeen is planned for 2010, in the Maritime Museum, as part of the Society's centenary celebrations. As a postscript on the subject of public exhibitions, the Society has a commendable record of support for national philatelic exhibitions. Donations or guarantees and contributions in the form of exhibits were made, for example, to the Philatelic Congress of Great Britain meeting in Margate in 1912 and in Harrogate in 1921, to the International Air Post Exhibition in 1934, to the British Philatelic Association meeting in Glasgow in 1947, to the London International Stamp Exhibition in 1950, to the proposed Scottish National Exhibition in 1966, to the SCOPHILEX exhibition in 1970, to the British Philatelic Federation meeting in Edinburgh in 1985 and to the Association of British Philatelic Societies' GLASGOW 2000exhibition. Aberdeen's location may have strengthened the case for local exhibitions in the past, but the Society has responded positively to requests for support of larger philatelic events elsewhere in the UK throughout its lifetime.

Chapter 7

The Growth and Demise of the Junior Section

In the very early years of the Society, prior to the first world war, no consideration seems to have been given to special provision for young collectors. "Any and all interested" were eligible for membership, without mention of age. It is likely that young collectors were admitted because a gold medal was donated to the Society by a Founder and one other member, to be competed for by Juniors.

At the AGM in 1919 a motion was adopted "that juveniles (those under sixteen years of age), in the event of a juvenile section being formed, shall pay one shilling per annum and that there be no entrance fee". A Junior Section was not yet formally in being, it seems, but three juvenile members were admitted after the exhibition in October 1919. One more joined during that season and towards the end of that same season a Juvenile packet was begun and members were invited to send sheets of stamps "for disposal only". At the 1920 AGM John Fraser was appointed to the newly created post of Superintendent of Junior Section. He was originally minuted as Superintendent of Juvenile Section, but the word "Juvenile" was deleted and replaced by "Junior" before it was printed in the syllabus, perhaps an early example of political correctness. The upper age limit was changed to eighteen and a month later a Junior Section Committee was initiated, not consisting of Junior members, of course, but of four Seniors "to make arrangements for the coming session regarding the Junior Section". These decisions proved to be well timed in that following the advertised public lecture by Fred Melville on the opening night of the 1920-21 season, nineteen boys were admitted as Junior members. The following season five of the eleven meetings were meetings of the Junior Section, with seniors and juniors each meeting once a month. Thereafter one meeting in each season was customarily scheduled as Junior Night, when the

Juniors displayed to the seniors. As from 1922-23 the Juniors met for half an hour before the scheduled meeting, although Juniors did then attend the main meeting of the evening.

From the outset a feature of the Junior Section was encouragement in the form of donations from Seniors, not least the gold medal whose whereabouts is unfortunately not now known. In 1922 the medal was awarded to Alan Fraser, age 14, who scored the highest aggregate mark in a three-part competition consisting of an essay on any philatelic topic, an exam on ten philatelic terms and an album competition. A manuscript copy of the examination paper survives, a challenge to any philatelist today! Needless to say, all of the six contestants received donated prizes.

A similar form of competition was instituted for the Juniors in the 1923-24 season when a question was printed in the syllabus for each evening meeting. The questions were mostly concerned with stamp design and the Juniors were expected to come to meetings with their answers in writing. The question for the opening night of the season was "On what stamp does the representation of an Aberdeen Steamer appear?". A question reading "What is reputed to be the rarest Stamp, and how was it produced" elicited nine correct answers, all receiving prizes, whereas a later question which asked the contestants to "Name the country which issued Stamps, one half of the stamps on the sheets being in one language, and the other half in another language" resulted in only one correct answer.

The Junior Section had its ups and downs during the inter-war years, with a rapid turn-over of members. Attendance was occasionally reported as disappointing or none too regular. A Junior sales packet was started in 1925 to encourage participation but sales were very low and it was abandoned. At the AGM of that year it was decided that "no special effort should be made on behalf of the Juniors meantime in view of the attractions of wireless"! Perhaps also relevant to the fortunes of the Junior Section was the formation of

Philatelic terms Exam. 22.2.22

1. Write the three words represented by the initial letters C.E.F.? (printed in black on King Edward VII stamps of India.)

2. What is a Surcharge.?

3. What do the watermarks CC and CA stand for.?

4. Write out in full :- O. W. OFFICIAL.? (This was printed in black on King Edward VII stamps of Great Britain.)

5. What is an Overprint? Explain by giving two examples on the Stamps of Gt. Britain King Geo V. Issue.

6. Explain what is a 'Burelé band.'?

7. What do you mean by the expression "Perf. 14."?

8. What is a Rouletted issue.?

9. On the foot margin of a sheet of Gt. Britain King Geo. Stamps, is the following :- M. 18 — what is the philatelic term for this and what information does it convey to Stamp Collectors.

10. What is the meaning of Line-Engraved.?

Questions on philatelic terms, compiled for the Juniors in 1922.

school stamp clubs at that time, most notably the Grammar School Philatelic Society which was described in the local press in 1923 "as responsible for a great philatelic revival" and published its own journal, "The Philatelist. The First Journal for Philatelists in the North, and Official Organ of the Aberdeen Grammar School Philatelic Society." The Junior Section continued in existence, nevertheless, and although Junior Night was no longer a regular feature of the annual syllabus of meetings as from 1926-27, it was reintroduced in 1933-34 as an evening event when several Junior members displayed to the seniors. In 1931-32 the ten Junior members were described as "very keen" with an average attendance of eight. In maintaining the Junior Section, the Society was expressly undertaking the function of providing instruction, although given that remit, it was not always easy to fill the post of Superintendent of Juniors and in the absence of a Superintendent, the Section was in abeyance when meetings resumed in 1941.

In 1944 it was agreed that Junior members were welcome to attend senior meetings, but no special provision could be made for them meantime. The following year a new Superintendent was appointed to reorganise the Section and over the next twenty years the Section was very successful. There were very large fluctuations in the Junior membership, with a peak of 120 in 1948-49 and with "the ever-growing number of Juniors attending the Senior meetings" debated (inconclusively) by the Committee in 1947. Assistants to the Superintendent were co-opted, with an average Junior attendance of forty in 1949-50, a year in which they visited the Post Office and Telegraph Department. In 1950 the main display at a scheduled meeting of the Society was given by T. Gordon Coutts, a 17-year old junior member whose collection had been awarded a silver medal, the second prize in the Junior Section of *The Stamp Magazine* 1949 Annual Awards Competition. He had been in hospital for ten months when he had entered the competition, which was for the best collection in one volume.

The Section became the subject of minor controversy at the AGM of 1953, when it was decided to omit the names of Juniors from the list of members which was printed in the syllabus. There was a long debate on the subject at the 1954 AGM, when a formal motion to reinstate the Juniors was defeated by eighteen votes to nine. That decision was unanimously overturned at the 1955 AGM and their names reappeared in the syllabus of 1956-57, only for the decision to be reversed at a Committee meeting in 1958 and for the list of Junior members finally to be omitted from the syllabus as from 1958-59!

The 1956-57 season was another good year for the Junior Section with an average attendance of thirty. There was support for school stamp clubs, with Walker Road Stamp Club attending the annual Junior Night. Possibly in consequence of the continuing success of the Section, there was inconclusive discussion in Committee of the age at which Junior members should be permitted to attend full meetings. At that same time a Junior member had asked to see the Packet, but it was ruled that members receiving the Packet must be twenty-one. There was, evidently, tension between the functions of encouraging the young collector and of respecting the wishes of more serious-minded seniors.

The Junior Section continued to flourish into the 1960s. Film strips were purchased for their benefit, later shown to the seniors. Support was provided for the then flourishing Mile End School Stamp Club and most of the sheets on display in the Society's permanent exhibitions were drawn from the Juniors' collections. In 1964 a 4-page Junior Newsletter volume 1, number 1 was produced but this seems to have been the only issue. The annual Junior Night continued to be favourably reviewed although the attendance of seniors was sometimes regrettably low. The seniors remained supportive in other ways, for example, twelve of the seniors gave displays at the thirteen Junior Section meetings in 1969-70. Junior Night in 1970-71 took the form of sheets which five Junior members had loaned for display. These were presented by the Convener of the

Junior Section who announced that he had informed the Juniors that they could leave when they wished, whereupon they all got up and left!

Attendance at Junior Section meetings declined in the early 1970s and never recovered, despite attempts to publicize the Society through school stamp clubs. At the 1972 AGM it was decided to leave the office of Convener of Junior Section in abeyance and to invite existing Junior members to attend senior meetings. Attempts were made, nevertheless, to continue to make special provision for Junior members but numbers had dwindled to no more than three or four and the future of the Junior Section was now a regular topic for albeit brief discussion at AGMs. By 1976 there were no Junior members. In 1990 a proposal made at the AGM to revive the Junior Section was discussed at length by the Committee. There were undertones of conscience in the discussion, in that the Society was no longer nurturing tomorrow's collectors. It was agreed that the Society should offer assistance to school clubs, but it was agreed not to attempt to revive the Junior Section.

The Junior Section in 1934, with the President, George Beverley, centre, and James Anderson, Superintendent of the Junior Section.

Chapter 8

The Library: Storage and Retrieval

The Society had already acquired the nucleus of a library by the time of the first General Meeting in 1910, when the President intimated that a Mr W.H. Peckitt[12] of London had sent the Society eight volumes relating to stamps and a Librarian was at once appointed. Since that early date, the maintenance of a philatelic library has been one of the functions of the Society, although its fortunes have fluctuated over the years.

Further donations followed during the first season, including Earée's *Album Weeds* in two volumes, and at the start of the second season a Library Committee of four persons was instituted. In 1912 the Committee responded to advice that a philatelic library which belonged to a Mr Alexander could be purchased at a price of £15, by recommending rather strangely that the Society contribute £5 towards the purchase price, with no indication of where the balance was to come from. The Society in full session debated the recommendation and accepted the original asking price. There is no clear indication of what was acquired in this purchase, but it probably constituted at least the core of what was to become a very significant library. At the same time, P.J. Anderson, Librarian of Aberdeen University, Vice President of the Society and a founder member, designed a book plate for use in the Society's library which is still to be found in some of the current holdings. The four corners were selected as representative of successful portraiture: Queen Victoria on the Black Penny of 1840; Washington on the USA 10c. of 1847; Hermes on the Greek issue of 1861; and the Prince Regent

---

[12]W.H. Peckitt was a stamp dealer in the Strand, who sold his business to Stanley Gibbons in 1913.

Luitpold on the Bavarian issue of 1856; while the border includes four varieties from the British Guiana provisionals of 1862[13].

As a professional librarian as well as a philatelist of international stature, P.J. Anderson may well have been influential in library matters in the early years. He was a signatory of the newly instituted Roll of Distinguished Philatelists in 1921, in recognition of his bibliographical work on early philatelic literature. At the opening meeting in 1911, P.J. Anderson had addressed the Society under the heading of "Notes on Early Philatelic Literature with Illustrations from the Aberdeen University Library". The talk was illustrated with about two hundred volumes from the University collections and a "Rough List" of these, in the form of a 34-page pamphlet was given to each member present as a souvenir of the occasion. A thirty-page "List of Exhibits" was published in Aberdeen University Library Bulletin 3 (1912). It was he who catalogued the library and framed the library rules, and as from 1912 the library was accommodated in Marischal College, in rooms formerly occupied by a late member of the Society, J. McLauchlan Young, Lecturer in Veterinary Hygiene appointed by the University in 1897.

---

[13]Anderson, P.J. 1924 "Scottish Philatelic Literature 1863-1923", *The Philatelist* 1, 9, 5-7.

A library catalogue was compiled and printed in the syllabus for 1912-13, together with Library Regulations. The library then comprised forty-three monographs, ten runs of periodicals mostly complete as at that time and fourteen runs of auction catalogues (including some long runs) and price lists. The monographs included such classics as Anderson & Smith's *Early English Philatelic Literature*, Hardy & Bacon's *The Stamp Collector* and Melville's country handbooks. The catalogue was printed in the syllabus on only one other occasion, in 1913-14, by which time three further monographs had been acquired.

One further occurrence in the affairs of the Library prior to the outbreak of the first world war was the appointment of the President, Secretary and Librarian as Trustees for the Library, although the reason for the creation of an office of trusteeship is not clear. It was evidently thought to be appropriate at that time.

In 1919 the library made the first of many moves, when it was relocated in the new meeting room in the YMCA. Some evidence of its utility is to be seen in that nineteen members borrowed seventy-two books in that season and concern was expressed about the dilapidated condition of some of the books and journals. The library and its bookcase were insured, nevertheless, for £100 in 1920. The catalogue was revised and printed apart from the syllabus, and placed on sale price 1/-, whilst a new venue for meetings that year necessitated the removal of the library to the Central School.

Accessions took several different forms in the early years. In 1915 the Society was given a collection of stamps picked up on the field of battle. An exchange of duplicate copies of philatelic magazines between the Society and the University's philatelic library was arranged in 1922. Seventy lantern slides were donated in 1924 and twenty-six more in the following year.

The 7-page library catalogue of 1920 listed eighty titles under the headings: Auction Prices, Bibliography, Biography, Catalogues, Collections, Colour, Congress Reports, Exchange Clubs, Forgeries, General Literature, Heraldry, History, Perforation, Periodical Literature, Poetry, Postmarks, Reprints, Specialist Handbooks.

In 1927, following a donation of the first five issues, the Society decided to subscribe to *The Scots Philatelist*, recently launched by the Junior Philatelic Society of Scotland. Periodical literature was very much a part of the library, but by its nature presented problems of storage and conservation, with consideration given to binding.

In 1925 the library suffered its first major loss. When the Librarian set out to remove the library from the YMCA to another new venue at 259 Union Street, he discovered that the bookcase had been forced and that books were missing. On checking, some thirty volumes appeared to have been stolen, including bound volumes of periodicals, Earée's *Album Weeds*, Hendy's *Early Postmarks of the*

British Isles, Melville's *Chats on Postage Stamps* and nine catalogues. The loss was reported to the Police but it seems that nothing was recovered and the Society continued to acquire literature which was to become collectable in its own right. For example, in 1926, a copy of Melville's *The Mayfair Find of Rare Stamps* was donated by P.J. Anderson.

In 1928 the library was removed to the Society's newly acquired premises in the Adelphi where a member provided a new bookcase. Most acquisitions were gifted, a haphazard process sometimes leading to duplication, and it was recognised that purchases were necessary to fill gaps. The library was certainly seen as an important feature of the Society's activities and it was enlarged in 1932 by a gift of the philatelic library of a late member, Miss Helen Donald. Other donations continued to be gratefully recorded sporadically, including the Arthur Hind sales catalogues and Warren's *Pageant of Civilization*. With hindsight it is evident that the Library was also growing as a financially valuable asset, emphasised by the purchase of *The History and Stamps of Ascension Island* published in an edition of 100 copies. The Librarian regularly reported increased borrowing by members in the 1930s, but equally regularly complained of members failing to return books when due.

The decision in 1937 to terminate the lease of the Society's rooms at the Adelphi and to hold meetings in the Caledonian Hotel put the future of the Library in doubt. The Committee decided that the matter should be decided by a full meeting of members and it was unanimously agreed "that the Society's stock of volumes be handed over to the Aberdeen Public Library". The Library's Trustees were asked for their written consent. The City Librarian had already indicated his readiness to accept the collection, an interesting indication of the status of the hobby at that time. The arrangements for the transfer were evidently very informal since there is no mention in the Public Library Committee minutes or in Society records of any conditions attached to the deposit, although the Public

Library minutes state that the reason for the Society's approach to the Public Library was "that the Society had agreed to disband"! This curious misunderstanding arose from a telephone conversation between the then Librarians. In any event, the collection, which amounted to 305 volumes and nineteen pamphlets, was removed to the Reference Department of the Public Library where it was available to readers. The Society's Office of Librarian went into abeyance at the 1938 AGM.

Although now out of sight, the Society's former library was not yet out of mind. In 1942 the Secretary asked the City Librarian for a list of the titles handed over and of any since acquired. At that time there was also a proposal to initiate a "Book Exchange" within the Society, but nothing seems to have come of it. Ten years later the City Librarian was again asked for a list of the books and also whether they could be housed in the Reference Room. The books were evidently no longer readily accessible, which may explain why they did now seem to slip out of mind.

One notable accession had occurred in 1947, however, despite the absence of a library at that time. Colonel H.W. Hill, author of *Rowland Hill and the Fight for the Penny Post* presented an autographed copy of his biography of his grandfather to the Society, the occasion being the loan to the Society by Col. Hill of the actual diploma awarded to Rowland Hill on his receiving the Freedom of the City of Aberdeen on 29 April 1844. According to the Town Council minutes, the honour was bestowed on him "as a mark of the sense entertained by them [the Town Council] in common with their fellow citizens of that gentleman's distinguished merit as the originator of the great and beneficial scheme of penny postage and the Provost was requested to transmit the diploma of Burgesship in name of the Council to Mr Hill". The signed copy of Col. Hill's book is still held in the library.

At the AGM of 1961 there was discussion of acquiring books for a library. It was decided that the Secretary would compile a list of books which members had indicated that they would be willing to loan. An announcement of the proposal was included in the syllabus of 1961-62 and a modest list of the offerings of four members was prepared. Then in March 1964, W.S.E. Stephen of Aberlour, a member of the Society, displayed "Russia" and in conclusion he donated autographed copies of his *Stamps of the Russian Empire Used Abroad* (with S.D. Tchilinghirian, 7 vols.) to the Society. Perforce, the Society was in possession of the nucleus of a library, courtesy of an eminent philatelist. At the AGM in the following month it was "agreed that a library should be started". A note was inserted in the syllabus of 1964-65 saying that "it had been agreed to form a Philatelic Library...to satisfy a long felt need..." and appealing for donations of books to the interim Librarian. Further signed donations from W.S.E. Stephen followed in the form of the classic *Austrian Post Offices Abroad* (with S.D. Tchilinghirian, 6 vols.) and purchases were made so that by the 1967 AGM, the Librarian reported "a very small nucleus on hand mostly given by Mr Stephen". Within five years there were sufficient accessions to justify the compilation of a modest library list extending to less than one side of a foolscap page. A continuing trickle of donations and purchases included *Gibbon's Stamp Weekly* vol. 11 (1910) in which the inaugural meeting of the Society was reported. Until 1971 the new Library was located in the Librarian's home, but with a new venue for meetings that year, the Library was relocated to Bon Accord House.

Another change of venue in 1978 coincided with the donation of a new purpose-made library cabinet. Lucky is the Society with a professional joiner in its membership! Accessions continued, however, and the growth of the Library is evident in a new list prepared in 1979, showing that the library had more than doubled since 1972 and by 1981 the library had exceeded the capacity of the new cupboard. This situation remained through the 1980s, despite continuing accessions and regular use by the membership. It was possibly the success of this revived facility which gave rise to discussion in committee in 1987 as to whether the former Society library might be retrieved from the City Library, but it was agreed that no action be taken "as title was probably lost after fifty years".

In 1992 the Society Librarian responded positively to an approach from Aberdeen University Library concerning the intended disposal of twenty-two bound runs of philatelic journals dating from 1866 to 1925 and amounting to some four metres of shelf space. These were journals which had been acquired and accessed by P.J. Anderson. The University recognised the associative value of the collection and wished to ensure that it was not split up. The Society could not undertake to house the volumes in the sort of institutional premises which the University Library Committee required, but fortunately the volumes are not lost to members of the Society or indeed to any other potential reader. Although the University Librarian did subsequently propose to authorise the sale of the collection "if this proves to be profitable", the provenance of the collection was drawn to his attention and no further action was taken. The journals remain in the University Library stacks.

Through the 1990s provision of increased storage space for new accessions was an ever-present problem for the Librarian, but the magnitude of that particular problem was to be dwarfed by events in 1999. The Librarian was alerted by the President to a list prepared by Aberdeen City Libraries which referred to "The Aberdeen and North of Scotland Philatelic Society Collection". A visit by the Librarian to the Public Library revealed that many of the titles were still in the catalogue. He contacted the City Librarian, expressing interest in the current status of the collection and its possible return to the Society. He learned that the collection was treated as one of the Special Collections in the City's Central Library where very little use had been made of it and that the City Librarian was quite willing for the collection to be returned to the Society. The formalities for the retrieval of the collection were a little more onerous than seems to have been the case in 1937, but they were readily completed and the Society Librarian removed the collection to his safe keeping on 18 November 1999.

The Society Librarian was then faced with the problem of amalgamating two collections and housing the enlarged library. He was authorised to dispose of duplicate items, as well as those that he considered not worth retaining, and members were given the opportunity to purchase surplus titles. A manageable collection of some 350 listed titles was rehoused in a substantial new cupboard, accessible during meetings and offering a remarkable reference facility to members. The collection continues to grow slowly, both by donation and purchase, and now contains both classic early works and some of the most recent philatelic research and reference publications. Those titles which spent sixty years in the professional care of Aberdeen City Libraries can still be identified by a Public Library bookplate recording their provenance.

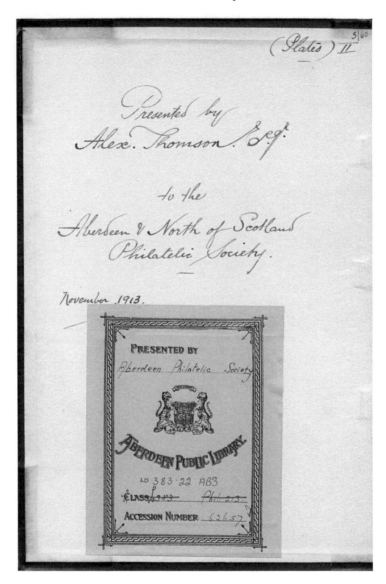

When the library was accessed by Aberdeen Public Library in 1937, bookplates were inserted, as in this example beneath the manuscript record of a title donated in 1913, namely Wright, H. & Creeke, A.B., *A History of the Adhesive Stamps of the British Isles*, 2 vols., 1899.

Chapter 9

Forgeries to Beguile and Deceive

The fascination with the darker side of philately, with the contest of wits between the knowledgeable collector and the miscreant who seeks to profit by skilful deception is almost as old as the hobby. The identification and collection of forgeries has long been practised, both to confound the perpetrator but also to amass and display spurious artifacts which are of interest in their own right. A reference collection of identified forgeries was thus begun in the very early years of the Society, whilst forgery and the forgery collection have on numerous occasions been subjects of entertainment in the Society's programme. The motivation behind the decision to accumulate the Society's collection is clear. It was perceived of as a virtuous activity which a responsible philatelic society should undertake. This was an attitude shared with the membership of other philatelic societies who also decided to compile forgery collections in their early years, e.g. the Scottish PS, the Caledonian PS, the Bath PS[14] and also the Dundee and District PS. The collections provided a source of reference which members could draw on to avoid being duped, but apart from a short period, the Aberdeen collection has not been extensively consulted for that reason. The collection has served primarily as a collection to be viewed with interest, and that seems to be the common experience.

At the second AGM of the Society in 1912 it was agreed to form a forgery collection. A curator was appointed to the post of "Expert" and members were invited to donate forgeries. By 1915 the rules of an "Expert Section" had been drawn up. Members were invited to

---

[14]Fleming, Ian J., 1993, *Scotland's First Philatelic Society 1893-1993*, Scottish Philatelic Society, Edinburgh, 8; Gardiner, Stewart, 2005, *The Caledonian Philatelic Society 1906-2006*, Caledonian Philatelic Society, Glasgow, 91-98; Hindley, Peter, 2006, *The Bath Philatelic Society 1906-2006*, Bath Philatelic Society, Bath, 14.

submit stamps for examination to the "Expert and Forgery Curator" and "his opinion will be given as to the genuineness or otherwise of the specimens submitted". It seems that items were submitted to him, but details of those early submissions are lacking, except that his work was reported in 1920 to be comparatively light. In 1921, however, he reported the examination of twenty genuine stamps, two forgeries and one bogus stamp. In the following two years he expertised ninety-six stamps and perhaps in consequence of the increased use of this facility, an Expert Committee was formally appointed in 1924. That committee was reconstituted annually until 1963, apart from the war years. Detailed records of its work are lacking and a proposal in 1931 that it be wound up suggests that it was not very active. In some years it seems not to have met, but small numbers of stamps were expertised in the post-war years. In 1952 it was said to meet "on occasion", but by 1956 formal submissions were no longer being put to the committee. It went into abeyance in 1964 and has not been resurrected, despite a proposal to do so as recently as 2000.

The Forgery Collection is of greater longevity than the Expert Committee and has increased in volume over the years, with no apparent connection to lack of consultation as a source of reference in the detection of forgeries. There was a stream of donated accessions in the early years, to the extent that in 1922 the Curator could report that he had "remounted the whole collection in a new album on loose leaves". The collection was displayed to the Dundee PS in the following year, when it was decided to enhance the reference value of the collection by adding genuine copies for comparison, and expenditure was authorised for the purpose. This proposal seems not to have been acted upon to any significant extent, because precisely the same proposal was put to the Society when the collection was displayed to members in 1938. Further expansion lead to the Curator remounting the whole collection once again in 1925. He also sought to exchange duplicate forgeries with other societies

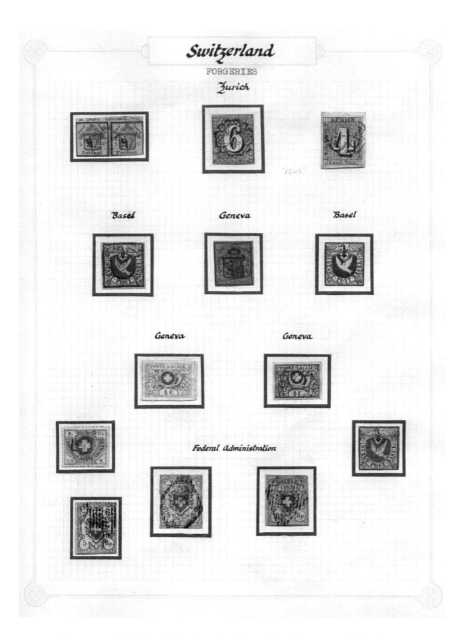

A page of Swiss Cantonals from the forgery collection.

and in the following year there was much interest among members in "a quantity of forgeries" presented to the Society. The collection, together with another collection loaned for the occasion by Messrs Godden of the Strand, were the subjects of an evening meeting in 1928. Donations continued and by 1932 the collection was said to total 662 items, "comprising 389 foreign, 138 British and Colonial, 135 bogus, 15 exhibition and 22 genuine Maltas".

Throughout the 1930s, accessions of forgeries from a very wide range of countries were gratefully received, including Sedang, Greece, Heligoland, Persia, Spain, Sicily, Brazil, German States, Paraguay, Bolivia, Griqualand, Argentina, Colombia ("a very fine forgery"!), USA, Surinam, Japan and the Ionian Islands. The collection was a prominent feature of the Society's exhibition in the Art Gallery in 1932. It was displayed again to the Society in 1935, and the manuscript of the Curator's address on that occasion is held in the archive. The collection had, by then, increased to over 800 items. The continued expansion of the collection was due, in no small part, to the work of George Milne, appointed when the collection was founded and still in office in 1938, twenty-seven years later, when he displayed the collection yet again to the Society. It was displayed once more to the wider public at the Society exhibition in 1943. In the post-war years there were further accessions of several large lots of forgeries, although in 1949 the Curator remarked ruefully that he had examined thirty-five stamps during the past year, mostly forgeries, but not one had been handed over to the Society's collection, rather implying that forgeries were becoming more collectable in their own right. That same year lantern slides were made of some of the forgeries in the collection, with a view to publication alongside illustrations of the genuine stamp, and in 1952 photographic enlargements were mounted as part of the collection now housed in three albums. By 1956 the collection amounted to some 1400 specimens and was insured for the first time for £100, the premium being 4/6d. Sadly, George Milne, the last surviving founder member of the Society, died in 1957, in his forty-sixth year of continuous stewardship of the collection.

In a press report of the Society's Jubilee exhibition in 1960 the second Curator stated that "it is a tradition in the Society that all stamp forgeries that come into the hands of members are handed over to the collection". A year earlier that same Curator had fallen in line with tradition by donating what had been his own private forgery collection to the Society, but thereafter donations appear to have become infrequent. Whether the acquisitions of members included fewer forgeries, or members were increasingly reluctant to follow the tradition is not clear, but by 1966 losses from the collection were causing concern. By 1970, however, the collection filled three and a half volumes.

During the 1970s the well-being of the collection became a subject of concern in the Society. Valuations ranged from £200 to £1000. There was concern about rising costs of insurance and it was deposited in the bank for safe keeping. The post of Curator was briefly in abeyance and at least a part of the collection was controversially issued on loan to an eminent member. In the absence of an inventory which had been proposed as long ago as 1964, a member volunteered to prepare a photocopy but was hindered by many hundreds of loose stamps. The three albums of mounted stamps were photocopied and made available as a catalogue in the Club library, so that members could readily identify any pages of particular interest to them, and the originals withdrawn from the bank for scrutiny. This facility was not utilised. With the appointment of a Curator in 1978 the collection was withdrawn from the bank, but during his sixteen years in office, the collection was by his own account "dormant". Although rarely, if ever, consulted by members, it was on display at ASPS Congress in 1985, as well as to the Society on opening nights of several seasons. In 1988 the Committee considered a proposal to dispose of the collection. The proposal was rejected on the grounds that it was a part of the Society's heritage.

Since 1992 the collection has been under the charge of one member who has tidied it up, given it an occasional airing, accepted the occasional donation and ensured that it can be consulted for the purpose originally intended.

GREAT BRITAIN

PENNY BLACK 1840

The left margin of this stamp has been added by an expert faker and forger, apparently by 'pulping' additional paper into the stamp along the left margin. The design (scroll work) is quite different, - compare the scroll-work on the right side. The Maltese Cross Cancellation has also been partly faked and partly forged, as proved by ultra violet radiograph by W. H. S. Cheavin.

The forgery collection includes examples of early line-engraved GB stamps which were examined by W. Harold S. Cheavin in 1948. W.H.S. Cheavin FRPSL was a chemist who designed a philatelic microscope in 1912 and carried out research into the use of ultra-violet light in philately. He published extensively on the application of the microscope to philately.

Chapter 10

The Exchange Packet: Trading in Duplicates

Philatelic Societies customarily seek to facilitate acquisition of stamps by members, although an exchange packet is something of a misnomer in this context. Members' duplicates are circulated around the membership and offered for sale at prices set by the vendors. They are traded for cash, not exchanged or swapped!

The decision to "arrange the working of the Stamp Exchange Packet" was taken during the Society's first season. The details of how it operated initially are not on record, but it was apparently successful from the outset. Rules were not formally drawn up and approved until 1913. They appeared in the syllabus for 1913-14, and they would still be familiar to anyone regularly receiving such packets today, except that stamps were mounted on sheets rather than booklets designed for the purpose. Dedicated stationery was purchased and the rules revised in 1915 when they extended to seven pages of the syllabus. It was one aspect of the Club's activities which continued through the war years, when apparently it did well.

The popularity of the exchange packet continued after the war, when five packets became the usual number to be circulated each season. A packet of twenty-four sheets which went into circulation in 1921, was valued at over £46, whilst the corresponding monthly packet in the year following contained sheets to the value of over £83, contributed by nineteen members. In 1923, however, the Secretary of the Exchange Packet Section reported several breaches of the rules, the most serious being an allegation of substitution of stamps in circulation. An elaborate "trap packet" was delivered to the suspect who subsequently was confronted, admitted guilt, paid for his ill-gotten gains as well as a fine of £2/10/0d. He was eventually struck off the membership list. The success of the packet continued. In the

1924-25 season the five packets contained 25,268 stamps valued at £420, of which 7,222 were sold for a total of £54.

The packet continued through the inter-war years with annual sales of around £100, a further revision of the rules and the intermittent circulation of a Junior Members' packet. It went into abeyance briefly on the outbreak of war, but resumed in the 1941-42 season in the face of difficulties of obtaining material and delays in circulation. Any such problems seem to have been resolved by 1948, with a noted improvement in the quality of material in circulation, and by 1952 twenty packets were in circulation. Sales were reportedly falling off by then, a trend confirmed in the 1952-53 season when another miscreant "took Exchange too literally and did a bit of swapping". Another trap was set but not sprung on this occasion.

THE ABERDEEN AND NORTH OF SCOTLAND PHILATELIC SOCIETY.

Sept Packet.

Received on 19.11.31 Despatched on 20.11.31

To Mr H.E. Wood. Cults.

Club Number of Sheet	Number of stamps taken	£	s.	D.	Club Number of Sheet	Number of Stamps taken	£	s.	D.
1	1	-	-	1	40		.	8	3
4	1	.	.	½	34	4		.	1
5	2	.	1	3	36	4			1
21	4	.	.	1	42	6		.	2
23	14	.	.	8½	47	9		.	9
25	6	.	.	1	48	4		.	3
29	1	.	5	9	51	1		.	1
31	3	.	.	1					
32	8	.	.	2	68		-	9	8
	40	-	8	3					

Signature, W. Marshall.

I hereby acknowledge receiving Sept packet this date

Date 21/11/31 Signature W. Dawson for Mr Wood

A control card for the Exchange Packet in 1931.

Continuing problems came to a head in 1955, when members complained about failures attributed to the Packet Secretary, and a succession of committee meetings followed. The Packet Secretary resigned and some terse correspondence was generated, followed by a short period when no packets were circulated. The packet was resumed under new management in the following year. At that time it was seen as an important link with members living as far afield as Shetland and the south of England, although the 1960s saw growing dissatisfaction among country members because of a shortage of packets in circulation. In 1966 no packets were circulated and thereafter it continued only in desultory fashion, not the least of the difficulties being the unfortunate death in office of two Packet Secretaries within five years and the resignation in 1968 of a recently appointed Packet Secretary. There were also problems of insurance and of insufficient and poor quality material. These and other problems were again debated by the Society in 1974 and an attempt was made to rejuvenate the packet in 1975 in the face of rising postal costs which had caused several country members to withdraw. In 1976 the committee debated the packet at considerable length and accepted that it was no longer viable. It was phased out over the 1976-77 season, with a postal auction proposed as a replacement facility for members to buy and sell stamps.

The problems that culminated in the demise of the exchange packet included the work load on the Packet Secretary, lack of good quality stamps on offer, prices which were too high, falling numbers on the circulation list and of contributors, as well as insurance and postal costs. What is not clear is why these problems arose, recalling the success of the packet in the early years. To what extent was the demise of the packet due to changes in the interests of members, as collectors became more specialised across a greater diversity of interests, including postal history and perhaps sought their acquisitions through more cost and time efficient sales outlets such as auctions? The post-1977 experience of this Society suggests that there is one critical problem which has to be resolved in achieving the viability of an exchange packet. The circulation by post of bulky packets containing large numbers of stamps of no interest to the subscriber is inefficient. This problem was addressed in yet another resurrection of the Society's packet.

In 1977 a member offered to supervise what he called a "sales box", an experiment whereby members' booklets would be made available at Society meetings. Sales amounting to some £250 in 1978-79 demonstrated the popularity of the new facility, and in 1988 the President was able to commend the growing success of the member who was once again entitled Packet Secretary. The system which he organised was much simpler than that which had been codified in 1913, which may be another reason why it continues as a low-key feature of most Society meetings, providing a service to a proportion of the members who make purchases, as well as to vendors, not all of whom are necessarily members. Vendors continue to pay a commission on sales to the Society as before. Members sometimes take the box of booklets home between meetings to go through it at leisure. The term "Exchange Packet" has slipped back into use, rather than "Sales Box", which was a phrase coined in recognition of a different system, but it is as much a misnomer as it was when it was first used!

Chapter 11

Auction Sales Take Different Forms

Sales of stamps by auction to collectors can be dated back to 1865, so it is not surprising that philatelic societies have organised auction sales for a very long time as another means for their members to buy and sell stamps. In the Aberdeen Philatelic Society, there is a long but sporadic history of auction sales organised in different ways. In 1913, however, the Committee considered "the advisability of having auction sales of stamps at some of the meetings but resolved not to proceed meantime".

In 1922 the sub-committee which drew up a programme of meetings included a stamp auction for the last meeting of the calendar year, with stamps on view from 8 to 8.45pm and John Reid as the first Auctioneer. The first auction was evidently a success. There was a large attendance of both Senior and Junior members and it was formally resolved to defer the reading of the minutes, etc., in order to allow as much time as possible for the sale of members' stamps. Fourteen members submitted 162 lots and 148 were sold. The total realisation was £27. 6. 2d, including 11/- for a mystery packet gifted by a member from Manchester. The highest realisation was £2 for "the £1 Georgian Great Britain". There was a proposal at the following AGM to hold two auctions next session.

Vendors at the two auctions programmed in 1923-24 were asked to send lots to the Auctioneer ten days in advance and a catalogue was prepared for the second auction that season. Lots offered for sale at the two auctions totalled 164 and 158, with realisations of £20. 13. 8d and £23. 13. 9d. Apparently, fine used British and British Colonial stamps all found buyers, whilst mint stamps did not find a ready sale and "a considerable number of lots" were unsold at the second auction of the season, when attendance was only "fair".

Thereafter auctions were an annual event for several years, with rather fewer lots than the first auction and total realisations ranging from £18 to £48. In 1928 the event was described in the syllabus as a "Dutch" auction of stamps gifted by members, with the proceeds to go to Society funds. Fourteen members donated sixty-four lots realising £7. 1. 7d, although attendance was affected by stormy weather. The following season the auction was conducted as in earlier seasons, but the popularity of the event may have been declining, with a "fairly good attendance" and forty-one of the sixty-seven lots on offer realising £10. 1. 6. In any event, the "Dutch" auction format with gifted lots was resumed for the next two seasons, with the 1931-32 sale benefiting the Society by £4. 16. 4 from the sale of seventy-four lots. The funds raised on that particular occasion were intended to offset a £5 subsidy of the "Majority Celebrations" dinner and dance which had been agreed at the previous AGM.

Only one further auction was programmed throughout the 1930s. In 1933, forty-seven of the sixty-nine lots on offer realised £4. 19. 3d. It rather looks as though the auction, as an event, had run out of steam.

The Society ceased to hold meetings with the outbreak of war, but the first full syllabus after their resumption included an auction as a means of fund-raising on behalf of the Red Cross. The intention was that both vendors and buyers should each contribute 2d in the shilling on purchases and sales. The auction was held in December 1942 and was an open meeting, not confined to members. It was attended by the Lord Provost who was also President of the local branch of the Red Cross. In the event, all of the ninety-eight lots were donated and all sold for a total of £18. 1. 0. A similar auction was organised a year later, when sixty-six sets of the Allied Military Government issue for Italy sold for 2/6 each and nineteen sets of "Free Norwegian stamps" were sold at a commission of 6d per set. In addition, sixty donated lots were sold and there were cash donations, the outcome being donations to the Prisoners of War Fund (£8. 5. 0) and to the British Red Cross (£23. 0. 3). One more charity auction was held, in

1944, when ninety-seven lots (or gifts, as they were described, hence probably not all stamps) realised £16 for the Red Cross. In peace time, auctions once again went into abeyance.

In 1950 the Committee drew up a list of conditions in preparation for a "Members' Auction Sale" which was to follow a display by a Junior member at the last meeting of that year. The display was warmly received but the auction which followed was not a success. There was insufficient time for all of the lots to be auctioned and only about half of those which were offered found buyers. If that was a test of the viability of auctions on a regular basis, then it clearly had a negative effect, as auctions ceased to appear on the syllabus for more than twenty years.

At the AGM of 1973, a member "proposed that the Society should hold an auction". The novel aspect of the proposal was that it should be held after the AGM in the hope that more members would attend that event. The proposal was referred to the Committee, which accepted it and met on two occasions to draw up guide-lines for the conduct of the event. Immediately after the 1974 AGM, 135 lots were offered for sale, £43.78 realised and a precedent set. Every AGM thereafter has been followed by an auction, consistently with good attendances and also ensuring that the business of the AGM is conducted expeditiously!

Auctions have been a regular and well supported activity of the Society ever since their experimental reintroduction in 1974, with the incidental benefit of a modest and regular income from 10% commission on sales. At the 1975 AGM, the auction which followed attracted "a full house". The magnitude of the event continued to be much as earlier, with eleven vendors offering 107 lots in 1976, when total sales amounted to £46. In that same year, the decision was taken to phase out the exchange packet over the 1976-77 season and particularly with the country membership in mind, an additional auction was introduced as a replacement facility for members to buy and sell stamps. This took the form of a postal bid sale and broke with tradition in one respect. The member who proposed it and offered to organise it, sought and was granted a free hand to proceed without reference back to the Committee for approval of rules and procedures. This was in contrast to past practice when lists of rules and regulations were drawn up, debated in committee and approved prior to implementation of auctions. It exemplifies a tendency towards a more relaxed and streamlined management of Club affairs.

LOT NUMBER	DESCRIPTION	ESTIMATE OR RESERVE(R)
1.	INDIA, 100 different, u. mostly KG V & KG VI	40p
2.	INDIA, p/s env, KG V 1a brown & additional adhesive, u. to Grenada	20p
3.	AUSTRALIA, 70 different, u. all reigns	30p
4.	CANADA, 90 different, u. all reigns	40p
5.	EUROPE, 50 different large commems.	30p
6.	GERMANY, Hitler skull, allied proaganda forgery "futsches reich", imperf block of 4, probably a reprint	60p
7.	PRINCE EDWARD ISLAND, SG 3, 6d blue, reprinted die proof(original die in RPS)	£2
8.	U.S.A., Eastman 3c 12/7/54, strip of 3 on FDC	20p
9.	DENMARK, "Thisted Filatelistklub" anniv. cancel(2) on stamped card, 7/10/62	30p
10.	N.ZEALAND, Telegraph Cent. 1962, pair on FDC	20p
11.	NETHERLANDS, 1st flight KLM Am'dam-Tokyo 4/12/51 cachet & b/s Tokyo arrival	70p
12.	GB, 2covers to Rotterdam 1918 labelled "Opened by Censor"	50p
13.	GERMANY, Ruhleben WWI internment camp. The complete collection of 16 stamps plus 2 blocks of 4(1 with double perf) un. except 1 block. Also 5 trial prints	R£20
14.	GB, 85 articles clipped from Stamp Collecting Weekly 1972-76	80p
15.	GB (MAP), Huntingdonshire by Lewis 1838 23 by 17 cm	£1
16.	CANADA, 1968 Nonsuch 5c in presentation folder	20p
17.	GERMANY (BOOK), "Luftpost der DDR" Leipzig 1960 illus. 139p. detailed	70p
18.	GERMANY, Philex Deutschland Color-Katalog 1971 simplified 124p. superb illus.	60p
19.	GERMANY, Michel Deutschland Katalog 1969, 381p. specialised	80p
20.	GERMANY, Bochum 650th anniv. cancel on 3 transport commems. 9/6/71	20p
21.	GB, 29/4/68 Bridges FDC	R30p
22.	GB, 15/1/69 Ships FDC	R80p

The first postal auction held in 1976.

This was a time when postal auctions constituted a growth area in stamp trading and the new postal auction proved to be successful at first attempt. Fifty-five lots were offered, of which forty-one sold for £26.30. The event was immediately repeated, beginning a sequence of two such events every season, a pattern which continues to be followed. The number of lots on offer rose rapidly, largely due to a very small number of vendors offering a large number of lots. Vendors who were, in effect, part-time dealers in a very small way, were attracted by an opportunity to reach a new market at no cost. If items did not sell, they incurred no charges.

Meanwhile, the number of lots at the room auction after the AGM rose, with 170 lots offered in 1978 and 137 in 1979. The evident popularity of the event lead to a proposal to add a mid-season auction to the syllabus, when there would be relatively little formal Society business, leaving more time to view lots and conduct the auction. Since 1979 it has become the practice for the last meeting of the Society before Christmas to be scheduled as a room auction. Attendance on the first occasion of the December auction was sixty, with some 230 lots realising over £300. From the outset, it was stated policy that room auctions should be light hearted affairs, as evident from the invitation to potential vendors in the Newsletter to look out the 1d black that the dog got hold of, or the tweezers with one prong missing. On one occasion a packet of "the new invisible stamp hinges" were on offer (presumably in a transparent packet). Vendors were discouraged from offering lots with high reserves, and many lots are sold for pence.

In recent years the two forms of auction have diverged to a degree, with the room auctions self-evidently directed at the membership, and the postal auction reaching a wider circle of collectors. In the case of the room auctions, vendors submit their lots at the start of the evening and are paid for sales (less commission) before the meeting closes. A limit on the number of lots per vendor was introduced in 1980, with a lower limit at the auction following the AGM. Procedures are informal, although a distressing incident occurred in December 1980, when several relatively valuable lots were stolen, inevitably leading to a review of the conduct of auctions. On that occasion the unfortunate vendors were immediately reimbursed by donations from other vendors and members. The numbers of lots on offer have declined slightly in recent years, but some 300 lots per year continue to be offered to members attending room auctions, including individual stamps, sets, covers, one-country accumulations, kiloware, literature, albums and stock books, even bottles of wine.

The postal auction has a more eventful history. The post of "auctioneer" changed hands on three occasions in 1978/79, but thereafter the auction increased in volume, with sales realising the order of £700 on each occasion by 1987. It was not necessary to be a member of the Society to participate in the postal auction. In fact, only a small proportion of the vendors and bidders were members and sales lists were mailed to anyone wishing to receive them, giving rise to the paradoxical situation of a member carrying out a Society function with a considerable work load, but that function used mainly by collectors who were not members, albeit providing an income for the Society. In 1990, with the retiral of the then organiser, it was decided that the postal auction should end, but this did not happen. Another volunteer stepped forward to maintain it. Then in 1995, when that organiser also indicated his wish to stand down, the lack of participation by members was again presented as cause for cessation, and it was again decided that the postal auction should be suspended. It seems, however, that the task of running a postal auction is something that appeals to collectors and within two weeks yet another volunteer stepped forward. The volume of sales rose thereafter, with more than 700 lots per auction and the annual income to the Society rising to as much as £300 in some years. With a further change in the holder of the office of Postal Auction Secretary in 2007, a high order of IT skills were brought to bear and the management of the postal auction was reorganised accordingly. The following year, a small team of interested members took over the operation which continues to provide a facility for collectors both within and outside the Society.

Chapter 12

The Social Scene

The Society was brought into being by serious-minded philatelists "to promote the study and practice of philately", and not for any wider social purpose. There is no mention of social occasions in the early years, apart from a dinner following the first AGM in 1911, an event apparently not immediately repeated. It was not until the Society was well established and functioning for its primary purpose that it was evidently thought appropriate to foster social contact in a more deliberate manner.

The first hint of a social event is in the syllabus for 1924-25, where the programme for one evening was entitled "Auction Sale and Social Evening". There is no mention of any social dimension to the evening in the minutes, but that event may have been the catalyst for the Executive Committee which drew up a programme for the 1925-26 season to include a "Social Evening" on 9 December. Close to that date, the event was deferred until an evening closer to the end of the session and a sub-committee appointed to make the arrangements. The event took place, not in the then regular meeting rooms of the Radio Society, but in the West End Café on Union Street, in March 1926. It was described as a "whist and social evening" and "a complete success", with seventy-one people present, presumably including relatives and friends, not just members. The experiment was repeated in the following season and was again "well attended and much enjoyed", in keeping with the popularity of whist drives as social gatherings which brought families together. A charge for admission was set to cover the costs.

A social evening when philately was not the main purpose was an annual event throughout the 1930s in various venues. Whist was the regular feature of the evening. In 1930, in response to a suggestion that dancing be included in the whist drive programme, it was decided that "no dancing be done but that a short musical interlude be arranged". The following season, two social events were organised, the first being a dinner and dance to commemorate the twenty-first anniversary of the foundation of the Society, a part of the "Majority Celebrations". Tickets, costing 7/6, were subsidised from the proceeds of a Dutch auction in the same season. The event took place in the Douglas Hotel on 23 October 1931, with a full report in next day's *Aberdeen Press and Journal*. The principal speaker at the dinner, the President of the Dundee PS, spoke of his two great disadvantages, that "he did not have the honour to be one of the group that lived in that well-known district, "twal mile roon and far are ye?"; also, "he was not a philatelist, he was a stamp collector". He went on to commend the "spirit of camaraderie which was the envy of all of the rest of the societies in Scotland". Incidentally, Aberdeen was described as the second youngest society in Scotland at that time.

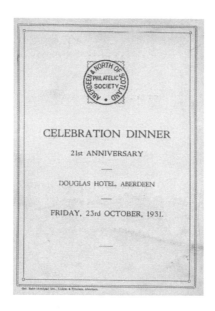

The 21st anniversary dinner menu.

That same season also saw the annual whist drive and supper in the Empress Café attended by about 100 members and friends, when the entertainment included songs and monologues. By 1934 the musical programme was regularly favoured by the inclusion of one member's "humourous items" (*sic*), whilst the award of a cheese to Edmund Bell at the 1935 event suggests further jocularity!

In 1935 the Society organised a Silver Jubilee whist, dinner and dance, very much as four years previously. The event took place on 11 October in the Royal Hotel. It was attended by seventy members and guests and again reported in the local press. The Society had attained their silver jubilee in the same year in which the King celebrated his and had accordingly telegraphed loyal greetings. A telegram was received from Sandringham in reply and was duly read out to the assembled company. On this occasion the President of the Dundee PS spoke of the friendly rivalry which existed between the two Societies, whilst a local speaker remarked on "how interest in their Society grew, in spite of fun poked at them by their friends". The budget for the event was finely judged. Tickets were again priced at 7/6 and the event again subsidised to the extent of £5 from Society funds. A 5/- menu was chosen and a band hired for £2. 2. 0., resulting in a surplus of 1/3d!

The usual social event was also held later that same season and continued in subsequent years, although a question was raised in 1937 as to whether "it was desirable to have the children". The main meeting agreed that the juniors be allowed to attend as in previous years. Then in 1938, it was decided, for reasons unknown, that there would not be a musical interlude. One can but wonder what form it had taken in the previous year.

The incoming President at the 1938 AGM declared that he would strive to increase the social side of the Society's activities and it was agreed that a dinner and dance should be arranged in the following session, but this decision was reversed in October of that same year

Members and guests at the Silver Jubilee whist, dinner and dance in 1935. Seated centre is the President, A.D. Imper., George Beverley, Past-Pres. seated right. Founder-member Edmund Bell is seated left.

by a majority preference for a social evening on the same lines as the previous year, that is, a supper and whist drive. The President was not to be denied, it would seem. A month later he intimated the date of 2 March 1939 for the Society's Social Evening and said that "it was intended to hold a whist drive, dinner and dance" with the price of tickets (5/-), double that of the previous year. There is, unfortunately, no record of the event and no syllabus was prepared for what would have been the 1939-40 season. In 1940 it was decided that no social meetings be held meantime and they were not resumed until well after the war.

A social evening was proposed at the 1948 AGM and scheduled in the syllabus for a date in December of that year. There were, however, problems in finding a suitable venue and it was held later in the season at the Bon Accord Hotel where the company was restricted to 132 persons. The event again took the form of a whist drive, on this occasion with a display of conjuring during the interval. In 1950 the second post-war whist drive was held in the Royal Hotel and "was much enjoyed", but for reasons unknown, that was to be the last social evening of the 1950s.

Resumption of social events was considered in 1955 and again in 1958, but it was not until 1960 that "lengthy discussion" gave rise to the decision in committee to arrange a whist drive in the 1960-61 season, when a beetle drive was in fact arranged. It was "a great success" and a "Beetle Drive" appeared in the syllabus for the next five years. Apparently, the punch which was served lived up to its name! Some sixty-four members and guests attended at first, but then attendance by members tailed off. The event was financially viable but increasingly relied on non-members to make up numbers, and after further straw polls of the membership, the beetle drive already in the syllabus of the 1966-67 was cancelled. It did not appear again in the Society's syllabus of meetings.

Aberdeen & North of Scotland Philatelic Society

BEETLE DRIVE

in the

VICTORIA RESTAURANT

on Friday 11th. March, 1966 meeting at 7P.M. for 7.30P.M.

Ticket 7/6

In the 1960s beetle drives replaced whist on social occasions

Social occasions of a different kind continued sporadically for a few years. In December 1969, at what would appear to be relatively short notice, the then Past-President proposed a dinner to celebrate the Society's diamond jubilee. This event took place at the Crescent Hotel on 9 April 1970, attended by forty-five members, guests and visitors. The menu was, of course, whimsically annotated with philatelic terms and the event seen as "a great success".

Members and guests at the Diamond Jubilee dinner in 1970. The President, Mrs. P.A. Orkin, is seated centre.

Two Fellowship awards in 1972 provided an appropriate context for another dinner which was held in the Pharos Restaurant on 28 November, with local press coverage. That event was repeated a year later when the thirty-four members and guests attending were slightly fewer than the previous year. The event continued annually in the same venue for the next four years, but declining attendance gave cause for concern. The dinners arranged in the 1976-77 and 1978-79 seasons were attended by some twenty-five people and in 1978 it was adjudged that there was little enthusiasm for the event and it was discontinued.

The award of Fellowships to Albert Smith, left, and E.W.S. Jupp, was the occasion for a dinner in 1972.

Much more recently a form of social event which reflects changed circumstances, has been an undoubted success, that is, the very informal fortnightly morning meetings, when ten or fifteen members meet for coffee and conversation, some of it philatelic. The rising age-profile of the membership and the relative ease of travel by public transport in the daytime perhaps explain this new form of social activity which would presumably have been inconceivable in the early years of the Society.

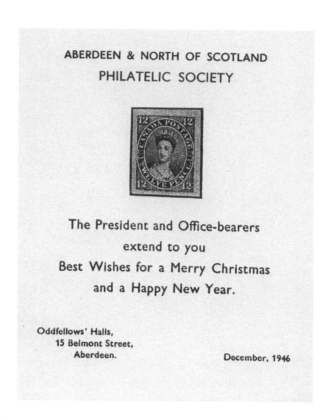

ABERDEEN & NORTH OF SCOTLAND
PHILATELIC SOCIETY

The President and Office-bearers
extend to you
Best Wishes for a Merry Christmas
and a Happy New Year.

Oddfellows' Halls,
15 Belmont Street,
Aberdeen.   December, 1946

A Christmas card when the President was an expert in Canadian philately.

Chapter 13

Publications: From Ephemera to Definitive Works

In a society whose founder members included the Aberdeen University Librarian, a scholar who published extensively and was posthumously referred to by Melville as "the bibliographer of philately"[15], publication was an activity to be encouraged from the outset. The membership of the Society has, over the years, included many philatelists engaged in original research who published their findings. Members have also been involved in the publication of philatelic journals of both specialist and general nature. A complete bibliography is beyond the scope of this work but some trends and significant titles can be identified.

Some of the meetings in the very early years of the Society took the form of lectures or papers which facilitated some form of subsequent publication. The most notable exponent was George Milne, whose researches were presented to the Society in the form of papers; drafts which were presumably read to the assembled company and later published in *Stamp Collectors' Fortnightly* and elsewhere. The same was true of some of P.J. Anderson's bibliographical studies. It was not only original research which was the subject of talks delivered at Society meetings and later published. A lecture entitled "Reminiscences of Fifty Years' Stamp Collecting", delivered to the Society in 1923, was published in *Stamp Collecting* (7 April 1923), in the form of a long résumé and provides insights into past collecting practices.

Not all of the early publications were serious, however. Another founder member, John Thomson Jr., was also one of the founders of a weekly Aberdeen journal appropriately entitled *Bon Accord*. He

---

[15]Melville, F.J., 1926, The Bibliographer of Philately. Sixty-five years as a stamp collector. *Stamp Lover* XIX, 2.

was said to possess a "great facility in the art of rhyme, and a sense of humour which has happily never deserted him". In the 1890s he removed to Sydney for health reasons but returned to Cove, Aberdeenshire, and in 1911, whilst an invalid, composed "a series of humorous poems, in all sorts of metre, dealing for the great part with stamps and stamp collectors". These were published in 1912-13, week by week in *Bon Accord* under the title of "Philatelic Frivolities", perhaps because the author had privileged access to the journal. Otherwise, their publication may be indicative of the status of the hobby, that they were considered acceptable for a journal with a general readership. They were surely not published on grounds of literary merit; perhaps better described as droll doggerel verse.

Mr. JOHN THOMSON, Jr.

The author of Philatelic Frivolities and the only bearer of the Society's short-lived office of Editor.

Philatelic Frivolities

By JOHN THOMSON, Jr.

No. XXI.

THE EXCHANGE PACKET.

Air—" THE TARPAULIN JACKET.*"*

A 'cute stamp-collector was eying
  Some " spares " on his table that lay:
And, some sheet-covers also espying,
  These sensible words he did say :—

Chorus—
  I'll send in some nice stamps to the Packet,
    Which the round of the members will go.
  And I hope they will all try to hurry up,
    For its progress is frequently slow !

Now, here's a stamp listed one shilling.
  Suppose I say eightpence for that.
This little reduction I'm willing
  To make on the price in the Cat.

Chorus—
We must cut down the price in the Packet, etc.

The first two verses will suffice! A bound volume of the complete series of poetical works by this author is held in the Society's library.

In January 1923 a member of the Society was instrumental in the publication of a little-known journal, possibly the first to be published in Scotland. It was entitled *The Philatelist. The First Journal for Philatelists in the North, and Official Organ of the Aberdeen Grammar School Philatelic Society*. It was edited by Alex M. Walker whilst a pupil at Aberdeen Grammar School, where he formed a stamp club in 1922 with the support of a teacher and members of the Aberdeen Society.[16] It ran for ten numbers in one volume, from January 1923 to August 1924. The sub-title changed three times to forms of words suggestive of a claim to unique status. In no. 4 (May 1923) the sub-title read *The First Journal for Philatelists and the only Scottish Philatelic Periodical. Circulated throughout Aberdeen Grammar School*; in no. 6 (August 1923) it read rather precociously *THE PHILATELIC JOURNAL OF SCOTLAND*; in no. 8 it read *THE FIRST JOURNAL FOR PHILATELISTS IN THE NORTH OF SCOTLAND, AND THE PHILATELIC JOURNAL OF SCOTLAND*. It attracted local advertising of a non-philatelic nature and the four pages of text in the first issue had increased to fifteen by no. 8. Contributors included P.J. Anderson, Frank Collie, W.B. Rawlinson and Frank Warren. The first two numbers were printed by The Granite City Press and thereafter by "Dingle, Printer, Plumstead, S.E. 18." The first eight numbers were published between January and November 1923, with two further issues in February and August 1924. The initial energy and enthusiasm was seemingly impossible to sustain. Extant copies must be very rare, the only known complete bound run being in the Society library, with an incomplete bound set in Aberdeen Central Library and another unbound in Aberdeen University Library. The Editor was a Junior Member of the Society for three seasons from 1923 to 1926. In 1938 he was ordained by the Church of Scotland, but demitted charge in 1950 to become a minister of the United Free Church because of what he believed to be the Church's policy of conciliation to the drinks trade. He changed his allegiance to the Free Church the following year and was readmitted to the Church of Scotland in 1954.[17] His energy as a young philatelist evidently remained with him later in life!

---

[16]Letter to the Editor, *Stamp Collecting*, 23 December 1922.
[17]*Aberdeen Journal*, 24 May 1954.

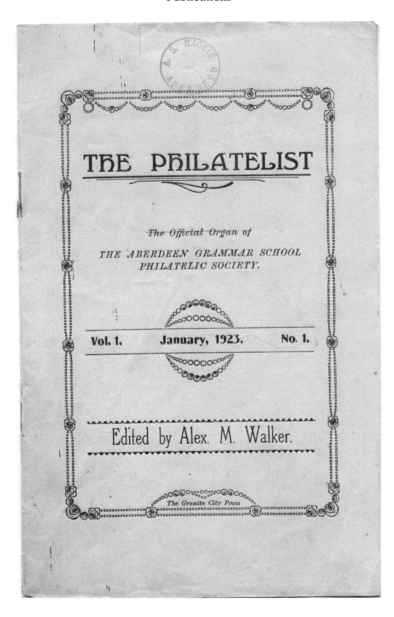

The first issue of "The Philatelist. The First Journal for Philatelists in the North....."

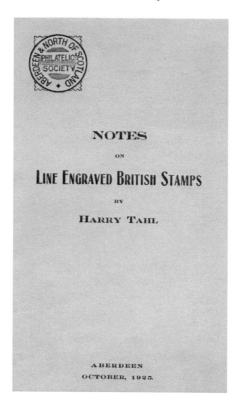

The first publication of the Society was the work of a member, a 16-page booklet in a first edition of 100 copies.

The Society has, on occasion, published in its own name, firstly in 1925. Harry Tahl, a member with a Glasgow address, displayed to the Society in four successive seasons from 1923, and the membership was greatly impressed by his four volumes of Great Britain line engraved. He had compiled "Notes on the Maltese Cross Cancellations" and offered to pass copyright to the Society if the Society undertook publication, which it agreed to do. In March 1924 a sub-committee was appointed and exactly a year later a printer's estimate of £10 was approved for an edition of 100 copies of what amounted to a 16-page booklet. In September 1925 it was decided that the price should be 3/- and that the Society should appoint Frank Godden as the London agent. Negotiations commenced, but meantime fifty-nine copies were sold by March 1926, almost recovering costs. A second edition of 500 copies was printed at scarcely more than the cost of the first edition. Negotiations continued with Frank Godden and an agreement was entered into whereby he purchased the entire second edition which he could sell at 1/6 each, except for fifty copies set aside for presentation and review. The Society profited by over £14 from the publication, but a curious feature was the title. The title of the original compilation was replaced by "Notes on Line Engraved British Stamps", something of a misnomer, as it is entirely devoted to Maltese Cross postmarks. A full-page advertisement for the first edition appeared in the 1925-26 syllabus, price 3/2 from the Secretary. The second edition was similarly advertised in the syllabus for 1926-27, published by Frank Godden, price 1/8, which must have dismayed purchasers of the first edition! The author offered to place further manuscripts dealing with British line engraved stamps at the disposal of the Society with a view to publication, but no action seems to have been taken.

Publication by the Society of the work of Tahl, a member resident in Glasgow, is indicative of the co-operation between the six Scottish philatelic societies in the 1930s. Reciprocity is evident in the publication of John Anderson's study of Scots Local Cancellations which was serialised in 1927 and 1928 in *The Scots Philatelist*, the official organ of the Junior Philatelic Society of Scotland (later the Caledonian PS). In 1929 the revised work was reprinted by the Glasgow society in a booklet which was marketed, price 1/6, by H.F. Johnson of Fleet Street, specialists in the stamps of Great Britain.

Shortly after the exhibition of December 1932, a short history of the Society by R.M. Lawrance was published in *Bon Accord*, noteworthy for profiles of past Presidents. It was privately reprinted in 1931 as an 8-page pamphlet in a limited edition.

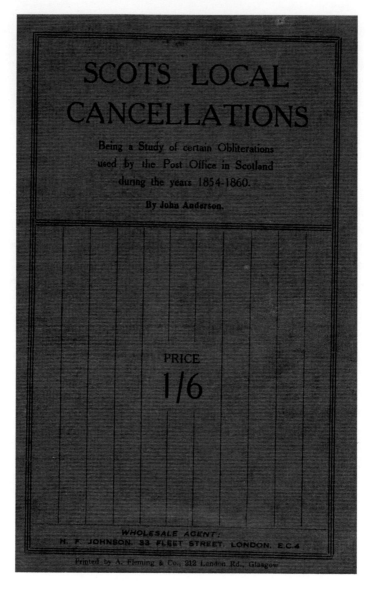

John Anderson's revised study of Scots Local Cancellations
was published in 1929, in a 35-page booklet.

The Society was represented at a meeting in Edinburgh in January 1932, convened to consider a proposal to establish a philatelic journal for Scotland, to be managed on behalf of all the Scottish societies which would accept financial liability. The Society agreed to support the venture and appointed a sub-Editor. The first issue of *Philately in Scotland* was published in April 1932, describing itself as the official organ of the six Scottish philatelic societies, including the Aberdeen and North of Scotland Philatelic Society. Edmund Bell of the Aberdeen Society was a regular contributor from the first issue, writing the Associate and Junior Section columns in the first four issues, before the Section was taken over by "Uncle Bill". Thereafter he continued to contribute on a range of subjects, latterly under the heading of "Things in General". Edmund Bell served on the Committee of the journal and in November 1933 he reported to the Society that the Committee "had agreed to admit contributed articles on "Postmarks" even though there was a feeling in the South against such", an interesting reflection on changing interests and attitudes within the hobby! *Philately in Scotland* ceased publication in December 1934 following the retiral of the Editor.[18]

Planned publications did not always materialise. In March 1914 it was agreed "that there be a magazine in connection with the Society". John Thomson Jr. was appointed Editor and promptly presented a medal in connection with articles contributed to the magazine, but the outbreak of war made it impossible to proceed. In 1935 the Committee decided that the society's history should be drafted and published as a brochure to commemorate the silver jubilee and a sub-committee was appointed for the purpose. The first minute book was handed to one of the then Vice-Presidents to prepare a draft, but four months later and in the absence of the author, the draft was said to be complete, yet no text had been received. There was an exchange of correspondence with the author,

---

[18]Gardiner, Stewart, 2005, *The Caledonian Philatelic Society 1906-2006*, Caledonian Philatelic Society, Glasgow, 77-78 & 117-120.

but no further action until April 1936, when the sub-committee met to consider "the notes compiled". The author had declined to continue to serve on the sub-committee and "in view of the lapse of time...expenditure...lack of enthusiasm", the sub-committee decided that no further action be taken. Reading between the lines, this rather looks like an occasion when members fell out and cross words were exchanged. Such occasions were perhaps not quite as rare as the formal minutes might suggest.

Another proposed publication which did not materialise, arose from a talk given to the Society by founder-member George Milne in 1946, when it was suggested that the Society should, for the benefit of members, finance the printing of the many lectures given to the Society by Mr Milne. The intention was reiterated in 1949, ironically in response to a talk to the Society by the member who failed to deliver the silver jubilee brochure, who was encouraged to combine his knowledge with George Milne in published form. These were proposals made in the course of votes of thanks and were probably more a measure of immediate appreciation than serious publication proposals.

Two Society publications which did materialise accompanied the exhibitions of 1948 and 1950. The provenance of these booklets are described elsewhere (see Ch. 6). The six short articles in the 1948 brochure are relatively ephemeral but the *ANSPEX Handbook* of 1950 included revised texts of the previously published work by George Milne on "Heraldry in Philately" and by John Anderson on "Scots Local Cancellations", as well as original accounts of the day-to-day working of the Down Special T.P.O. by W.A. Fleming, the postal history of Aberdeen by W.L. Falconer and forgery detection by Dr V.M.M. Watson.

With the approach of the Society's 75th anniversary, a member took it upon himself to edit a commemorative publication with only occasional recourse to committees by way of courtesy, something which would probably not have been possible in the more formal context of earlier years. Entitled *The Northeast of Scotland - A Philatelic Miscellany*, it included original work on Post Office mechanisation, railway postal history in Grampian, Scots local namestamps and a profile of P.J. Anderson. In the absence of recent work, W.A. Falconer's "A Short Postal History of Aberdeen" (1950) was reprinted. The 63-page book was printed in an edition of 350 copies and published at the 1985 annual Congress of the Association of Scottish Philatelic Societies in Bridge of Allan, price £3. It sold out within months and a loan of £400 from the British Philatelic Trust to assist publication was repaid. It was reviewed in sixteen philatelic and non-specialist journals and newspapers; it was awarded a bronze-silver medal in the 1985 British Philatelic Federation exhibition and was the first recipient of the ASPS Robson Lowe Literature Award in 1986. One other publication commemorated the 75th anniversary, namely, a postcard depicting Aberdeen postmarks which sold in excess of 1,200 copies.

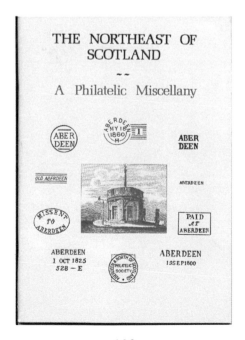

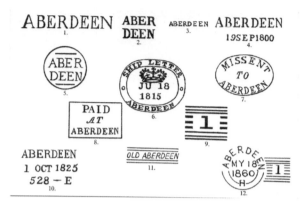

Postcard commemorating the 75th anniversary of the Society.

In 1966 the Society's Press and Publicity Officer suggested a Newsletter for country members who derived little benefit from membership if they were unable to attend meetings. The Committee costed and approved the proposal "after a full discussion", and two newsletters (not entitled as such) were compiled with the "out-of-towners" in mind. The first was circulated to country members only and was apparently well received, since there was a response of some thirty letters to the Editor, mostly seeking advice about the Society or other philatelic matters. The second 2-page circular was compiled with country members in mind, but was probably circulated more widely through the membership, leading to the compilation of a third 3-page "NEWS SHEET" in that same year, not obviously directed at country members and again circulated more widely. The Press and Publicity Officer declined nomination at the 1967 AGM and it fell to the Society Librarian to compile a "Newsletter" for full circulation in September 1967. It was reproduced by means of Gestetner stencils. Because of problems of access to a duplicating machine and because it was "difficult to get any material", the Newsletter went into abeyance.

At the 1969 AGM it was decided that there should again be a Newsletter which the Press and Publicity Officer agreed to compile. Two Newsletters were circulated in the following season, a pattern which has been followed with great regularity ever since. The informal post of editor ceased to be associated with the office of Press and Publicity, becoming a dedicated function in its own right and initially with frequent change in the volunteers. For some years it was compiled by the Secretary and in recent years it has been associated with the post of Delegate to the Association of Scottish Philatelic Societies, who has information to convey on a regular basis. From the outset, it was apparent that the editor could not anticipate frequent voluntary contributions by members to fill each 2-page issue. It is incumbent on the editor to seek out suitable subject matter and to draft the text. It continues to serve as the means of communication between the committee and the membership, with a regular paragraph from the Treasurer. It welcomes new members, records the wider philatelic achievements of members, reports on ASPS Congress and SCOTEX, publicises local stamp fairs, comments on national and international events, and indeed on anything else of philatelic interest that the editor happens to be aware of. The archived file of Newsletters is a useful additional source of information on the history of the Society.

Individual intentions to publish are perhaps more easily brought to fruition than committee-based decisions, and in the 1960s the Society took pleasure in the publication by W.S.E. Stephen (with S.D. Tchilinghirian) of their monumental studies of the *Stamps of the Russian Empire Used Abroad* and *Austrian Post Offices Abroad*. There have, of course, been many other significant original contributions to the literature of philately by members of the Society (see Appendix), most recently *The Postal Markings of the Gambia 1858 to 2000* by Stewart P. Duncan (with Oliver Andrew). Members have also made recent contributions of an original nature to the journals of specialist societies and study groups including *Maple Leaves, The India Study Circle Journal, The Scottish Post,*

Scandinavian Contact, The Finnish Philatelist, The Cinderella Philatelist, The London Philatelist, Journal of the Forces Postal History Society, Postscript and *Cameo.*

Philately in Scotland, first published in 1932, was the official organ of six societies in Scotland, including the Aberdeen and North of Scotland Philatelic Society.

Chapter 14

Publicity and the Media

The formation of the Society in 1910 was widely reported in the philatelic press and in the local press. Thereafter reports of meetings were sporadically published for many years, at times more consistently than others. A long 3-column report of the Presidential Address to the Society in 1923, entitled "Eighty-three Years of Stamp Collecting", appeared in the *Aberdeen Journal*, an indication of the potential interest in the hobby amongst the readership of a daily newspaper, whilst further reports of the meetings in that year were published in *Stamp Collecting Fortnightly*. In 1926 *The Scots Philatelist* commenced publication and although it was the official organ of the Junior Philatelic Society of Scotland, it regularly published reports of meetings by other societies, including Aberdeen.

The first issue of *Philately in Scotland*, published in April 1932, included a report on "Philately in the North". Thereafter the Aberdeen Society regularly contributed to the "Reports from Scottish Societies" column. In 1934, the year in which *Philately in Scotland* ceased publication, *Stamp Magazine* commenced publication and carried reports of Society meetings including Aberdeen, as did *Philatelic Magazine* from 1935. In the late 1930s reports of meetings of the Society were regularly published in the *Evening Express*.

The Press and Publicity Officer continued to submit reports of meetings to the press for publication after the war with some success, although in 1948 and 1949 he complained to the AGM about reports being cut down in the local press and of periodicals which failed to print reports. Nevertheless, short reports of 100 words or so were published regularly in the local press in the 1950s, sometimes picking out curious facts or events for the headline, e.g. "Apologies from P.O. - In 1800". A much longer advance report resulted from the well-advertised talk by Robson Lowe in the Music Hall in 1952,

RARE ITEMS SHOWN TO PHILATELISTS

ABERDEEN SOCIETY MEETING

Interesting and rare exhibits of pre-stamp covers were shown at a meeting of Aberdeen and North of Scotland Philatelic Society by Mr William Marshall, Belmont Castle, Meigle. The rarest item shown was a Glasgow cover, dated 1769.

As many authorities claim that 1774 is the earliest known date of a Scottish postmark it will be realised that Mr Marshall's exhibit is unique.

An envelope, dated "Aberdeen, 1788," along with postmarks of various types and colours also attracted interest. Many covers showed curiously named Scottish post offices, now defunct. A good example of these was an envelope marked "Scouring Burn," Dundee, 1850.

Mr Marshall concluded his display on a modern note by handing round for inspection a collection of air mail covers, many of them first flights.

Mr H. M. Wallace, president, was in the chair, and Mr John Anderson expressed the great interest derived from the lecture and exhibits. On the call of Mr John Fraser a vote of thanks was accorded to Mr Marshall.

Report of a meeting of the Society (*Evening Express* 3.12.37), characteristic of regular press reports in the late 1930s.

under the headlines "The Kings' Stamps - Lecturer to Show Reproductions". In 1953 it was the treatment of reports by the philatelic press which caused the Publicity Officer to complain: "scant reports of meetings or none at all". By 1955 it was agreed that "sending reports to the philatelic press was useless" and was ended. Local press coverage was, however, increasingly worthwhile and throughout the late 1950s and early 1960s, press coverage was described as excellent, as a result of good relations established by the Press and Publicity Officer with a columnist of the *Evening Express*.

By 1967 local press coverage was much reduced, for no stated reason, and the Press and Publicity Officer discontinued his reports to newspapers and journals "as so few were published". His resignation may be indicative of his lack of enthusiasm for the post, because three years later the *Evening Express* was again regularly reporting meetings, although philatelic journals remained less receptive. Good local press coverage continued throughout the 1970s, with occasional photographs of special events and with reports latterly submitted by the Secretary in the absence of a Press and Publicity Officer, a post which was not easy to fill. Reports to the *Evening Express* were abandoned abruptly in 1981, however, as a security measure following theft from a Club auction. In 1987 a post of Publicity Officer was recreated, but with little continuity. The Society's name reappeared briefly in the Club page of the *Evening Express*, but regular publicity in the local press, local radio or the philatelic press has not subsequently been achieved. Perhaps the most significant event in terms of publicity in recent years was the creation of the Club's website[19] in 2006.

Members have occasionally promoted the hobby to a wider audience. In October 1923 the Assistant Station Director, Aberdeen Broadcasting Station, briefly addressed the Society and "stated that he would be pleased to grant facilities from time to time for a fifteen to thirty minutes talk on Stamp Collecting". The President, Edmund Bell, gave a "Stamp Talk" from the Aberdeen Station on 7 December, followed by George Milne whose talk on "How Stamps are Printed" was broadcast early in 1924, and by Dr Peter Howie whose "talk on Stamps" was broadcast on 26 April 1924. George Milne also broadcast on stamp collecting in Childrens' Hour in the early days of the Aberdeen Station. Much later in 1956 Dr V.M.M. Watson was complimented on his recent broadcast on philately. In 1977 four members were invited to represent the Society on a BBC radio programme entitled Club Call, and in 1994 a team of three

---

[19] www.aberdeenphilatelic.org.uk

members entitled "Aberdeen Philatelics" narrowly lost a contest with Spey Valley Rotary in the Top Club 94 series broadcast by Grampian TV.

Three members represented the Society in a Grampian
TV quiz programme in 1994.

Since the 1930s the hobby has also been promoted by members through talks to professional and adult-education groups such as Rotary and PROBUS. Recently a member developed a slide-talk for such occasions, perhaps inappropriately entitled "Philately will get you nowhere"!

A logo bearing the name of the Society and designed like a circular postmark first appeared on the syllabus in 1911 and continued to adorn the syllabus until 1956, when it was replaced with a reproduction of the 1d black. The two devices had both been used on the soft cover of the ANSPEX Handbook of 1950. The circular logo was used on publications, dinner menus, certificates, etc., but it began to fall out of use long before the change in the name of the Society made it obsolete. The cover and insert designed for the ASPS Congress of 1967 incorporated a reproduction of the Mercat Cross, briefly the site of Aberdeen's Post Office from 1821, and that outline now appears on stationery, certificates, exchange packet booklets, the postal auction catalogue, etc.. It seems that it has, perforce, become the Society's logo, despite brief use in the 1970s of a rather uninspiring picture of another early Aberdeen post office building, the Adelphi Post Office of 1840-42 (see p.33). A rubber stamp of the original logo is retained in the archive.

The design of the Golden Jubilee Exhibition publicity label was adapted from labels used to publicise the 1948 and 1950 exhibitions, incorporating a logo in use since 1911.

The Mercat Cross logo with the original title of the Society.

founded
1910

The Mercat Cross logo with the amended title of the Society

Press photography (1981) is helpful publicity but groups are usually posed by a professional photographer in a way that bears little relationship to the conduct of Society meetings.

Chapter 15

Wider Participation

At a committee meeting of the Society on 2 September 1921, a letter from the Secretary of the Dundee and District PS was read on the subject of a "Scottish Congress and Exchange of Papers on Philatelic Subjects, etc..". The committee responded by proposing an exchange of visits between the two societies, something of a *non-sequiteur*! The two Societies in Edinburgh and Glasgow apparently responded more specifically to the proposal and agreed a venue[20], but there is no record in the minutes of the Aberdeen Society that this meeting took place.

On four occasions between October 1922 and February 1923, the committee considered correspondence from the Secretary of the Dundee Society dealing with the arrangements for the forthcoming visit to Dundee. At the same time, arrangements were being made for a reciprocal visit by members of the Dundee Society to Aberdeen in March 1923. There was indeed an exchange of visits by members of the two societies in February and March 1923, but the visit by the Aberdeen Society to Dundee was in fact a part of a joint meeting of the four Scottish societies. The joint meeting held on 17 February 1923 was fully reported in the philatelic and local press[21] as a very successful event. Several members from each of the four societies gave displays, including Aberdeen, and it was decided that there should be an annual meeting of a similar nature. That did not happen in 1924, however, when the Philatelic Congress of Great Britain was held in Glasgow.

---

[20]MacKenzie, George, 1990, In the Beginning, *The Glasgow Thematic Society hosting The Association of Scottish Philatelic Societies 61st Congress...*, Glasgow Thematic Society, Glasgow, 18-19.
[21]"The gathering of the Clans", *Stamp Collectors' Fortnightly*, 3.3.23; "£2500 stamp in Dundee", *Dundee Courier*, 19.2.23.

The wording of the Aberdeen Society minutes make it plain that a "Meeting of representatives from the Scottish Societies on 28 February 1925 in the premises of the Dundee Art Society" was convened at the instigation of the Dundee Society. "A number of members intimated their intention of visiting Dundee". Joint meetings were held in Glasgow in 1926 and in Edinburgh in 1927, but there is no formal record in the Aberdeen Society minutes of attendance or involvement, perhaps because these meetings were seen as the responsibility of the host societies rather than formally involving all of the Scottish societies. The Dundee Society again took the initiative in 1928 by making the arrangements for a joint meeting in Perth. The Aberdeen Society was asked to appoint a delegate "to read a paper" and to nominate members "prepared to bring collections for exhibition". Edmund Bell agreed to read a paper and four exhibitors were identified. Eight members attended from Aberdeen and reported enthusiastically on the meeting "as the finest of its kind yet held in Scotland". It was decided that Perth should be the venue in future and a representative committee of the Scottish societies was appointed, so that the event no longer relied on the initiative of one or other society.

Edmund Bell was the first Aberdeen representative on the Committee of the Joint Scottish Philatelic Societies. The joint meeting in 1929 was chaired at the nomination of the Aberdeen Society by the then retiring President of the Aberdeen Society, John Anderson. The practice that had become established was that the Presidents of the several Scottish societies took it in turn to preside at an event which rather resembled society meetings, except for a meal provided for all participants. Each year the organising committee of what became known as "The Perth Meeting" selected a continent to be the main focus of exhibits during two sessions, with an additional session when specialised collections were available for inspection at leisure[22]. There was certainly regular attendance at the event by

---

[22]Kidd, A.E., 1932, "The Perth Meeting", *Philately in Scotland* 1,1, 7.

members of the Aberdeen Society, although the record is not detailed since the organisation of the event was not formally a part of the business of the Society. In 1930, however, twelve members apparently took advantage of special party rates negotiated with the Railway Company of 11/3d per head.

A matter which was formally considered at a meeting of the Aberdeen Society in 1934 does indicate a major difference between the conduct of the event at that time and the way in which it subsequently evolved. The Society was asked to consider a motion that there should be no sales or dealing in stamps in the room where the conference is held and that the trade must make other arrangements for their accommodation, a far cry from today's trade-dominated event. After full consideration the Aberdeen delegate was "instructed to favour continuation of buying and selling at the Conference, except between the hours of 3 and 4pm". The delegate later reported the decision of the organising committee to permit dealing between 11 am and 3.45pm; also from 5.15pm onwards. The continuing commitment of the Society to the Perth Meeting is evident in the decisions by the Committee in 1934 "that expenses be paid yearly to approved delegates attending the meeting of arrangements for the Perth Conference" and that Society Secretaries should receive agendas in advance of the organising committee's meetings, so that "delegates may be instructed". The Aberdeen delegate reported regularly thereafter. Then, in 1935, the Society was levied 16/8d by the organising committee for the purchase of the frames used at the event, which had previously been loaned by the organising Secretary. A passing reference to "the Society display" for the 1939 meeting suggests that all of the participant societies regularly contributed to the event.

In 1940 the Society was consulted concerning the advisability of holding a Congress that year. The view of the membership on what had by now become known as the "Annual Congress of Philatelic Societies in Scotland" was that it should be cancelled, which indeed happened. Later that year the Committee decided not to send a delegate to a proposed meeting to consider the question of future Congresses. It was not until 1945 that a proposed revival of the Perth Congress in 1946 was put to the Society committee, which was in favour.

The revival of the Perth meeting seemingly lead to a proposal to form an "Association of Scottish Philatelic Societies" and the appointment in 1946 of an Aberdeen delegate, O. A. Fraser, "to any subsequent meeting". The Association was inaugurated, not without opposition, on 25 May 1946. Later that same year, the Aberdeen delegate was elected to serve on one of the standing committees. The Association assumed responsibility for the annual joint meeting of Scottish philatelic societies which had resumed in that year but was not always to be held in Perth thereafter. In 1950 the meeting took place in Glasgow and in the following year in Bridge of Allan. Names of people attending were sought in advance by the organisers, a function performed by the Secretary of the Aberdeen Society but numbers are not on record.

In March 1952 the committee convened to consider "a matter of precedence" arising from the Society's responsibility for the annual Congress in 1953. The point at issue was the nomination of the Congress President and it was agreed that the Society's Vice President and President-elect, John Petrie, should be nominated as President of the Association and hence preside over Congress. It was also decided that the event should take place in Aberdeen. The event was held in the Music Hall on 4 April 1953, with a pre-Congress dinner in the Douglas Hotel on the previous evening, an occasion which was well supported by Congress members from the south and by members of the Aberdeen Society. Next day, a room in the Music Hall "was filled to overflowing" for the Presidential address to Congress. Fourteen of the nineteen Scottish Societies were officially represented. The expenses of Congress in Aberdeen were born by the

Aberdeen Society and a week-long exhibition was staged in the same venue (see Ch. 6).

Member's badge made for the 1953 Congress of the Association of Scottish Philatelic Societies, the only occasion when Congress has been held in Aberdeen.

Consideration was given to hosting Congress in Aberdeen again, in the Society's Jubilee year of 1960, but it was decided not to proceed so that 1953 was the only occasion when Congress was held in Aberdeen. The following year, Congress returned to Bridge of Allan where eight members of the Society were in attendance and the President expressed his pleasure that so many members from Aberdeen were present. The Congress Secretary's report in 1954 acknowledges "the great goodwill and immense generosity" of the Aberdeen Society in meeting all of the costs of the 1953 Congress. It seems that Congress was previously in some financial difficulties and was restored to a sound financial position in 1954 thanks to "hospitality from the Granite City" in the previous year. In recent decades it has become the practice for the membership of the "host" society to provide displays and for one of its officers to preside over

Cover commemorating the Congress of the Association of Scottish
Philatelic Societies in 1967 which was hosted by the Society.

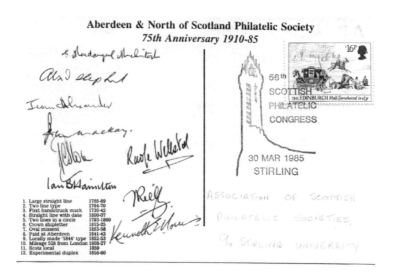

Postcard commemorating the 1985 Congress of the Association of
Scottish Philatelic Societies, signed by office bearers and guests.

both the Association and its Congress for one year, with a permanent venue reducing the logistical problems of staging an exhibition. In 1967 the Society hosted Congress and J.J. Waterman was President.

Then, in 1985, the Society again hosted Congress, as part of its 75th anniversary celebrations, when the event was held at the University of Stirling, with Dr G.M. Mackintosh presiding. In 2002 Congress relocated once again, this time returning to Perth, where the duties of the host Society now include the arrangements for the Tom Rielly memorial lecture and display and for the speakers at the annual dinner, as well as providing displays during the two-day event. The Aberdeen Society looks forward to hosting the event in 2010 as part of its centenary celebrations.

Apart from the Society's participation in the Association of Scottish Philatelic Societies and its forerunners, it has also supported organised philately at the national scale. After the foundation of the Society in 1910 it immediately joined the short-lived Postage Stamp League (see p.3). At least as early as 1922, the Society subscribed to the Permanent Congress Executive Committee, the organisation founded in 1909 for the purpose of meeting annually under the title of the Philatelic Congress of Great Britain. The Society responded positively to a request for its co-operation in the mounting of the 1924 Philatelic Congress in Glasgow. It is not clear whether the Society continued to support that organisation in a tangible manner, but it certainly gave financial support to the 22nd Philatelic Congress held in Bath in 1935, and two members sent sheets for display at that event. A decision was taken after discussion not to affiliate to the 28th Congress in 1946, perhaps because of the imminent formation of the Association of Scottish Philatelic Societies at that time. The Society held preliminary discussions with a view to hosting the Philatelic Congress of Great Britain in Aberdeen in 2010 but decided not to go ahead on the grounds that the event was not of great interest to the membership.

The Society was affiliated to the British Philatelic Association from June 1948 and was listed as such in the BPA Directory. The annual payment of the affiliation fee was unquestioned until 1977, when reservations were apparently expressed in committee concerning affiliation to the British Philatelic Federation. Despite further reservations the following year, the Society maintained its affiliation until the demise of BPF in 1993. The Society was represented by its delegate in discussions within the Association of Scottish Philatelic Societies of the need for a new national body and of its funding. The Society decided not to affiliate to the newly formed Association of British Philatelic Societies in 1994 and confirmed its decision in 1995, but the following year it decided to affiliate as from 1997 and has remained an affiliated society since then.

Chapter 16

Honours, Awards, Memorials and Insignia

The original constitution of the Society drafted in 1910 includes an Article headed "Honorary Members" which reads rather strangely today, perhaps reflecting the *mores* of times past. It states that original (presumably founder) members shall be enrolled as honorary members on retiral and that subsequent members shall also, on retiral, be eligible for election as honorary members. The reference to retiral is presumably from membership of the Society, as though anticipating that with advancing years members would inevitably be unable to participate in the activities of the Society. The same article in the constitution also empowered the Society to "admit any person interested in Philately, as an Honorary member".

Honorary Membership was invested sparingly. Former President James Anderson is listed as the Society's first Honorary Member in the syllabus of 1922-23. Thereafter, only nine more persons were elected as Honorary Members up to 1948. Not all of them were previously paid-up members of the Society but were presumably persons held in high regard for various reasons, and they included two spouses.

Elections seem to have been made occasionally in the past to honorary posts which were not specified in the constitution. When the AGM of 1920 elected James Anderson "an Honorary President of the Society" in recognition of services to the Society through his ten years as President, the constitution then in force only made provision for a category of "Honorary Members" without reference to any particular office. Then, in 1921, P.J. Anderson was elected Honorary Vice-President and in 1922 he was elected an Honorary President along with James Wood. In 1923 the post of Honorary Vice-President, which had been declared vacant at the AGM of 1922, was abolished, despite the fact that there seems to be no record of it ever being formally created! The abolition of that honorary office did not stand in the way of the unanimous election of J.H. Stephen as Honorary Vice-President in 1932. In fact, from 1920 until 1946, several elections were made to honorary presidential and vice-presidential posts at AGMs. In the 1920s, it became the practice that Presidents, on retiring from office, were accorded the status of Honorary President, until 1932 when they began to be listed under the heading of Past Presidents. Thus the non-constitutional designations of Honorary President and Honorary Vice-President were seen, seemingly, as the appropriate accolade to honour members. Members honoured in this way remained on the list of members and presumably continued to pay membership dues, an admirably Aberdonian device! A more formal mechanism to honour individual members was established shortly after the second world war.

At a committee meeting in May 1946, it was remitted to a sub-committee of six to "consider in what manner suitable recognition be given for meritorious service to the Aberdeen PS or the cause of philately in general". Subsequent proceedings were handled with much formality. The sub-committee met twice and drafted a new Article for the constitution, whereby any Member of the Society who may have shown outstanding merit in the conduct of its affairs may be elected to Fellowship of the Society and creating a Fellowship Awards Committee. In January 1947, the committee received the draft and called a Special Business Meeting of the Society later that same month, when motions and amendments were debated and put to the vote before it was decided that no further action be taken until the forthcoming AGM, when the new Article 14 was incorporated into the constitution and the Awards Committee was elected. At that point, the AGM was formerly adjourned until the first scheduled meeting of the Society in the forthcoming season. This was a procedural device to allow the new Awards Committee to take prompt action in selecting members for the new award. One hundred Certificates of Fellowship were printed and on 9 October 1947, prior to the first meeting of the 1947-48 season, the AGM was reconvened. Orations were delivered and Certificates of Fellowship were presented to three eminent members.

When first instituted, the Fellowship Awards Committee evidently dealt with something of a backlog of worthy nominees and within ten years, nine members had been honoured in this way. The bye-laws require that the number of Fellows shall not exceed a specified small percentage of the total membership of the Society and only one further member was nominated in the next ten years, with two members finding themselves listening to orations in both 1969 and 1972. Since then there have been five further awards, most recently in 2004, and the certificate has been redesigned. Thus, there are nineteen names in total on the roll.

In 1985 the Society was advised of a bequest from a late Fellow of the Society, Edgar Jupp. The committee was undecided over the most appropriate way to commemorate the generous donor and the matter was raised at the next AGM, when many members favoured the purchase of a trophy. The committee then took the decision to use the entire bequest to purchase a handsome hallmarked silver quaich which became known as "The E.W.S. Jupp Award". The trophy has been awarded annually at the discretion of the committee, either for the best display in the past season by a member or for services to the Society, with the names of recipients again inscribed on a roll, as well as on the base of the trophy.

In 1985 the Society was advised of a bequest from a late Fellow of the Society, Edgar Jupp. The committee was undecided over the most appropriate way to commemorate the generous donor and the matter was raised at the next AGM, when many members favoured the purchase of a trophy. The committee then took the decision to use the entire bequest to purchase a handsome hallmarked silver quaich which became known as "The E.W.S. Jupp Award". The trophy has been awarded annually at the discretion of the committee, either for the best display in the past season by a member or for services to the Society, with the names of recipients again inscribed on a roll, as well as on the base of the trophy.

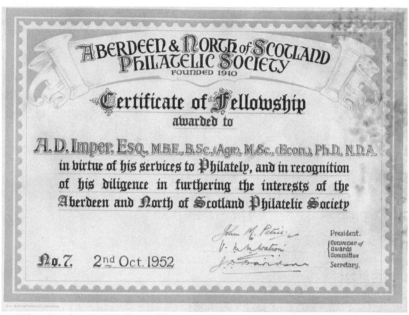

The Society's Fellowship certificate, as originally designed.

The E.W.S. Jupp Quaich

On 18 March 1954, John Anderson, who had joined
the Society in 1911, gave a talk and display to the
Society, entitled "Reminiscences of an Old Timer".
Following the vote of thanks, Mrs Anderson was
presented with a bouquet of flowers in a china basket
in recognition of Mr. and Mrs. Anderson's 38th
wedding anniversary, and John Anderson was
presented with a personal philatelic momento!

In 1982 A.S. Mackie gave a "Jubilee" display, the anniversary being
his fiftieth year of Society membership, an occasion which was
marked by a presentation, whilst at the AGM of 1984, a presentation
was made to celebrate fifty years of Society membership by A.H.
Beattie. Longevity is happily evident amongst the membership. Like
most societies, incidentally, the Aberdeen PS regularly presents a
certificate by way of appreciation to both visitors and members who
display to the Society (see p.123).

In 1982, A.S. Mackie, centre left, gave a display to the
Society during the fiftieth year of his membership, an
occasion which was followed by a presentation.

A modest world collection was bequeathed to the Society in 1994 by
Paul Everatt, a member for a number of years. The collection was
sold and the realisation used primarily to acquire a lectern with a
suitably inscribed plaque, an item of furniture which continues to be
in regular use. One other small item of furniture was acquired by the
Society at a much earlier date. During his Presidential years in 1960-
62, when the conduct of meetings was more formal than in recent
years, A.S. Mackie felt the need of a gavel to bring meetings to
order. His friendly contacts with the patternmakers at Hall Russell's
Shipyards were put to good effect and a fine gavel was forthcoming.
It remains in use, frequently and vigorously on auction nights.

Many societies of long standing also possess some form of presidential regalia, usually a chain of office. This has been an oft-debated topic in the Aberdeen PS. It was first proposed for consideration in 1951, but the committee was concerned about the cost and took no action. It was proposed again in 1953. A meeting of the committee was convened solely to consider the proposal and decided unanimously against. In the aftermath of the Jubilee dinner in 1960, when visiting society Presidents wore their chains of office, the acquisition of a similar item of regalia was again proposed. The then seventeen surviving Past Presidents were envisaged as possible benefactors. The proposal was regularly carried forward in committee until in 1965, the Lord Lyon King of Arms was consulted over design, and costing for a medallion was obtained but in 1966 it was considered to be out of the question. In 1985 some modest form of regalia was again proposed, but once again the committee decided not to proceed. Then, in 2007, a motion was put to the AGM proposing the acquisition of a Presidential medallion, but the motion was defeated and there the matter rests.

There is also a long history of recognition of members of the Society by outside bodies. Four members have been invited by the Association of Scottish Philatelic Societies to sign the Book of Scottish Philatelists[23] and the same number have received the Association's Award of Merit[24].

The highest accolade, however, dates to May 1921, when P.J. Anderson was invited to sign the Roll of Distinguished Philatelists, in recognition of his bibliographical work on the history of philately. He was named alongside such philatelic luminaries as Edward Bacon, R.B. Earée, Louis Hanciau, John F. Luff, F.J. Melville and P.L. Pemberton, one of twenty-five distinguished philatelists whose names were inscribed on the Roll in the year of its inception.

---

[23] John Anderson, W.S.E. Stephen, A.S. Mackie, J.C. Stone.

[24] A.S. Mackie, J.J. Waterman, J.C. Stone, Mrs S. Den.

John Anderson . M.B.E.

Mr John Anderson, M.B.E. has been invited to sign this book to keep on record the very outstanding work he has done over many years to encourage all forms of interest in Philately in Scotland. He will be particularly remembered for his careful work and original research on Scottish Local Cancellations, culminating in his classic book on this subject.

John Anderson

April 1964

John Anderson was the first signatory of the Book of Scottish Philatelists in 1964. The book was brought to Aberdeen for purposes of signing the citation.

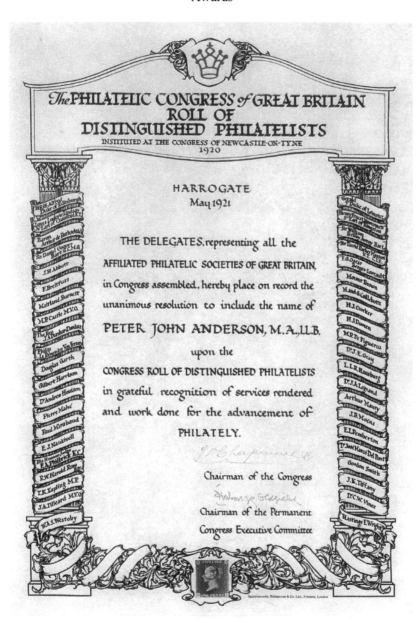

The PHILATELIC CONGRESS of GREAT BRITAIN
ROLL OF
DISTINGUISHED PHILATELISTS
INSTITUTED AT THE CONGRESS OF NEWCASTLE-ON-TYNE
1920

HARROGATE
May 1921

THE DELEGATES, representing all the
AFFILIATED PHILATELIC SOCIETIES OF GREAT BRITAIN,
in Congress assembled, hereby place on record the
unanimous resolution to include the name of
PETER JOHN ANDERSON, M.A., LL.B.
upon the
CONGRESS ROLL OF DISTINGUISHED PHILATELISTS
in grateful recognition of services rendered
and work done for the advancement of
PHILATELY.

Chairman of the Congress

Chairman of the Permanent
Congress Executive Committee

P.J. Anderson's RDP scroll is now in the Society's archive

The Society submitted the name of another founder member, George Milne, on three further occasions, without success. Incidentally, in May 1920, the Society had vigorously debated and adopted a response to the inception by the London Stamp Club of the Order of Philatelic Merit, from which the RDP evolved. The Society clearly felt itself to be a part of, and contributor to, the national philatelic scene from that early date.

It has been said in recent years that Aberdeen is not a competitive Society, but over the years members have competed, not so much among themselves, but at national and international exhibitions. The record is incomplete, but some of the events which have attracted the participation of Society members are known. The earliest is the eleventh Philatelic Congress of Great Britain in Glasgow in 1924, not exactly a competitive event, but one where George Milne was awarded the Telfer Cup for the best of the seven papers. A member from Ballater, Col. A.E. Stewart, achieved a high award for his study of the Indian _ anna of 1854-55 at the 1933 WIPA exhibition in Vienna. Members were successful at the Cairo exhibition of 1946, at CAPEX, Toronto, in 1951 and at Cape Town and Utrecht in 1952. Then, over the next three decades, a small group of members who were researching the stamps of Canada were regularly gaining trophies and awards from the Canadian PS of GB. They also gained several awards in STAMPEX in the late 1970s. The Admirals Cup of the Canadian PS of GB has been won by a Fellow of the Society on no less than seven occasions.

Research and publication in the 1980s resulted in literature awards to members in the form of a Scottish Postal History Society trophy, the ASPS Robson Lowe Salver and awards at the British Philatelic Exhibition and Cardinal Spellman Philatelic Museum; more recently, the Norden award of the Scandinavian PS. Two members have twice been awarded the ASPS Ferris Trophy and elsewhere at national level, members have exhibited successfully at STAMPEX and at the ABPS biennial exhibitions, both individually and through the Inter-

Federation competition, as well as in Scandinavia. Six members displayed at GLASGOW 2000 when awards to members included gold. At the international level in recent years, members have achieved commendable awards for exhibits at NORWEX 97, LONDON 2000, STAMPEX 04, ESPAÑA 06 and NORDIA 06. In a "non-competitive" Society, members continue to participate in national and international exhibitions where assessment is by grade rather than against other philatelists.

HON. MEMBERS

1922-39 James Anderson
1924-30 Wm. J. Riddell
1926-69 John A. Reid
1932-62 Mrs William Marshall
1933-39 Dr J. Wilson Clyne
1933-52 Mrs James Anderson
1933-37 John Thomson, Jnr.
1933-48 Andrew Gray
1934-39 James Paterson
1947-72 Mrs Annie Anderson

HON. PRESIDENTS

1920-32 James Anderson
1922-26 P.J. Anderson
1922-32 James M.A. Wood
1925-32 W. Edmund Bell
1926-32 Dr Peter Howie
1928-32 George Milne
1929-31 John Anderson
1930-32 William Ferrier
1933-34 R. Murdoch Lawrence
1946-47 W. Edmund Bell
        W.A. Fleming
        James Shand

HON. VICE-PRESIDENTS

1920-22 P.J. Anderson
1932-42 Dr J.H. Stephen
1933-42 R.W. Sherrit
1933-46 James Shand
1937-42 W.A. Fleming

THE E.W.S. JUPP AWARD

1986 D.A. Macdonald
1987 J.J. Waterman
1988 J.R. Little
1989 J.T. Gawthorpe
1990 N. Lutwyche
1991 A.S. Mackie
1992 A.D. Kindley
1993 J. Kyle
1994 J.J. Waterman

FELLOWS

1947 Edmund Bell
     George Milne
     John Anderson
1948 John Fraser
1950 Dr V.M.M. Watson
1951 Charles A. Wilson
1952 A.D. Imper
1955 O.A. Fraser
1956 W.L. Falconer
1959 Hector Monro
1969 J.B. McKenzie
     A.S. Mackie
1972 Albert Smith
     E.W.S. Jupp
1981 J.J. Waterman
1984 Dr G. McD. Mackintosh
1989 Bruce Walker
2003 J.C. Stone
2005 A.L. Walker

THE E.W.S. JUPP AWARD

1995 J. Clark
1996 R.A.Stables
1997 J.C. Stone
1998 S.P. Duncan
1999 A.L. Walker
2000 T.L. Beedie
2001 Mrs S.M. Den
2002 E. Vase
2003 F.C. Jefferies
2004 G. Alexander
2006 A.G. Wilson
2007 Ms A. Simmers
2008 N. Lutwyche
2009 D.A. Macdonald

P.J. Anderson, RDP

Chapter 17

Financial Affairs: Prudence Prevails

In the early years of the Society, the Treasurer's report to the AGM was regularly "considered satisfactory". This would seem to have been a modest understatement. In the very first year, the annual subscription was set at 2/6d but there was also a surprisingly high admission fee of 5/- which may, in part, account for income exceeding expenditure by some thirty percent. A continuing satisfactory balance allowed War Savings Certificates to be purchased and the Society emerged from the war years with a credit balance. In 1921 the Treasurer reported a deficit for the first time and the annual subscription was raised to 5/- (the admission fee had been halved in 1919). Remarkably, the debit balance was actually advanced by the Treasurer himself and the Committee then proposed a *café chantant* to raise funds, but it had to be abandoned through lack of support. The following year the Treasurer again reported an albeit smaller debit balance, and the Committee was required "to consider ways and means of reducing abnormal expenditure". The members of the Committee responded by subscribing the amount of the deficiency from their own pockets and by the next AGM the Treasurer was able to report a healthy credit balance.

Thereafter, the financial situation seems to have improved, in that later in 1922, a Housing Fund was established and one half of new entrance fees were allocated to it (the other half to the Library Fund). The acquisition of rooms in the Adelphi in 1928 and the financial commitment involved necessitated a review of the Society's financial situation. The first rental was paid from the Housing Fund, but that fund was dissolved and the sums remaining transferred to a new Reserve Fund. An auction sale of stamps donated by members was held as a means of increasing income, and money was gifted towards the costs of furnishings, but the hire of dedicated rooms was evidently straining the budget, since shortly after the acquisition, the

Committee agreed that it was imperative to sub-let one of the two rooms acquired. By 1929, however, the financial position of the Society was "sound" and the eventual decision in 1937 to relinquish the lease was not for financial reasons.

The financial position of the Society in the inter-war years remained sound. Regular income was sufficient to meet an occasional deficit on social evenings and in 1936, the Society donated five guineas to the Lord Provost's New Infirmary Appeal Fund. In 1938 the Society's "highly satisfactory" credit balance resulted in the purchase of £50 War Loan on behalf of the Society. In 1940 the Society purchased £25 of 3_% War Stock "on favourable terms" and the Society continues to hold £75 of 3_% War Stock to this day, with the appropriate interest accruing annually.

The annual membership subscription of 5/- as set in 1921 was unchanged for twenty years. No subscriptions were charged in 1940-41 and in 1941 a reduced war-time subscription of 2/6d was set, at a time of fewer meetings. The subscription was restored to its previous level in 1946 and retained at that level for a further decade, a measure of the continued growth in membership. A formal proposal to raise the very long-standing subscription of 5/- to 7/6 was put to the AGM of 1952 but was voted down. The annual balance nevertheless remained in credit, although in 1956, an office bearer pointed out that the Society would shortly be drawing on reserves to meet current expenditure, but it was not until 1957 that the annual subscription was raised to 7/6d. The entrance fee was abolished at the same time. In consequence, the cash in hand at the end of the financial year doubled, with a further small boost to income from a decision to invite advertising in the syllabus.

More recently, increases in the annual subscription are a reflection of inflation, reduced membership numbers and alternative sources of income, principally auction commission. In 1971 subscriptions were raised to 75p and a new category of members residing outwith ten miles from Aberdeen was created, subscribing 50p. Increases were more frequent through to the 1990s. In 1976 the main subscription was raised to £1.25. In 1980 it was raised again to £1.50, with the country membership redefined to 20 miles outwith Aberdeen. In 1982 the two categories were raised to £2 and £1 and in the following year the main membership fee jumped to £3. In 1992 the two categories were raised to £5 and £2. Then in 1997 the main category was raised to £7. Ten years later it was raised to £10, mainly due to increased room rental.

After the second world war occasional donations continued to be made to good causes, including the Red Cross and the F.J. Melville Memorial Fund, but prudence was also evident. By 1950 the rising cost of advertising meetings in the local press was considered to be exorbitant and that form of publicity was discontinued.
In 1958 the Committee decided to launch an appeal to members for contributions towards the additional costs envisaged in the forthcoming Jubilee year and £25 was immediately raised, increasing to £87 from other sources within a year. At the AGM of 1961, the Treasurer reported that £55 remained after all the Jubilee year expenses had been met and it was decided to retain the Jubilee fund in a separate account. A proposal that the fund be invested was not acted upon and since that time, the Jubilee Account has remained a regular item in the annual accounts. In its early years the sum increased modestly by the amount of interest accruing, but in 1970 it was drawn upon to support the exhibition and dinner in celebration of the Society's Diamond Jubilee. This usage evidently created a precedent, because in 1972 it was again drawn down to its post-1960 level, this time to support a dinner to mark the award of two Fellowships. Through the 1970s, the fund again increased solely by interest accruing, although in 1985, there was an increase in the interest added, when the account became the temporary home for a legacy and also a loan from the British Philatelic Trust in support of the 75th anniversary publication. In 1988 it was agreed, but not implemented, that the account be renamed the Centenary Account

and thereafter the account has provided a useful home for earmarked funds and for the occasional transfer of reserves from general funds into an interest bearing account. It remains a modest nest egg or pump-primer in applications for financial support as the Society looks towards its centennial year.

The balance of general funds over the past four decades has remained consistently favourable and stable, no doubt a reflection of good stewardship by successive Treasurers. A feature which Treasurers have regularly drawn attention to, is income from auction commission, which has sometimes exceeded income from subscriptions. Major items of expenditure and income are relatively predictable, hence budgeting is not hazardous. There have, of course, been occasional unpredictable incidents such as a proposal in 1963 to award honoraria to the Secretary, Treasurer and Packet Secretary, a suggestion which did not find favour. In 1977 the Treasurer announced the good news that HM Inspector of Taxes had decided that assessing the Society for chargeable profits "is not now an economic proposition"! In 1980 a separate subscription for Junior Members was abolished. Income from that source had never been significant. It was never more than seven percent of subscription income, even when numbers were at their highest. It had always been set at a low level, of course, but the Junior Section was no longer functioning by then. The British Philatelic Trust briefly provided financial support for visiting speakers to Aberdeen PS in the 1980s, a cost which has always been relatively high by virtue of the Society's location. In the late 1990s, what was termed a "voluntary levy" of £1 on top of the annual subscription, was introduced briefly in support of the GLASGOW 2000 exhibition. The costs of celebrating the Society's centennial are not entirely clear at the time of writing, but additional funds are being raised and will surely be put to good use.

Chapter 18

Constitutional Affairs: The Light Touch of Good Governance

On 13 April 1910, the newly appointed Committee of the Society met to draw up the Constitution and Rules of the Society. Judging by the minutes, the purpose of the meeting was achieved with remarkable facility, bearing in mind the impressively detailed document which was emerging. A week later the draft Constitution and Rules "were carefully gone over and unanimously adopted" at a General Meeting of the newly formed Society. The fourteen Articles of Constitution headed Name & Objects, Membership, Suspension or Expulsion of Members, Management, President, Secretary, Treasurer, Meetings, Subscriptions, Honorary Members, Resignation of Membership, Change of Address, Official Organ, and Amendment were circulated in the syllabus of 1910-11 and in the following two years. Minor revisions were made in 1913, none of any substance, and the revised version appears in the syllabus for 1913-14, the last year in which the Constitution was included in the annual syllabus.

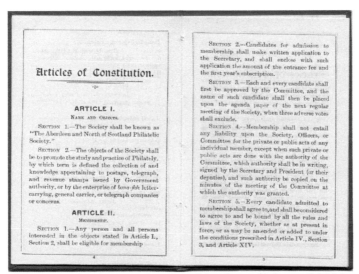

The constitution as circulated in the syllabus of 1911

The original constitution, as formulated by our founding fathers, continues to exert an influence on the affairs of the Society a century later. There have, of course, been amendments. They have been much abridged. What were separate Rules for related activities such as the Exchange Packet, were incorporated into a single constitution for a long period, but reading the most recent form of the constitution adopted in 2009, the elements remain and the terminology of the original draft is still echoed in a modern context. The importance of strict adherence to every letter of the constitution is no longer rated so highly in conducting the business of the Society, of course, and the interpretation and use of the constitution has changed over time. For example, the Article empowering the President to appoint Standing Committees is little used by comparison with the early years. Indeed, it was removed altogether as part of a constitutional revision in 1936, which also simplified the conduct of meetings and resulted in a revised booklet including the Articles of Constitution as well as the Rules of the Exchange Packet, the Expert Section and the Library.

A Library Committee was instituted in 1914 and then a plethora of committees was created in the years immediately after the First World War. In 1920 an Expert Committee and a short-lived Club Rooms Committee came into being, followed by a Permanent Collections Committee, a Junior Section Committee and Library Trustees in 1921. In 1923 the Permanent Collections Committee and the related Curatorship were abolished, in effect the reversal of a previous decision to form a permanent collection, and the Library Committee was also abolished, leaving a body of elected Library Trustees to fulfil the function. Then, in 1924, the Junior Section Committee was abolished, leaving only the Expert Committee and the Library Trustees to be elected at the AGM. Thereafter, such committees as were occasionally created, were not so much Standing Committees as provided for in the constitution, but *ad hoc* committees concerned with particular events, for example, social occasions, exhibitions or amendments to the constitution. The Expert

Committee lingered on precariously for some time. Proposals in 1931 and in 1960 to dissolve the Committee, presumably because of lack of business, were not acted on, but it finally went into abeyance in 1967, although the office of Curator of the Forgery Collection continues. The function of Library Trustees was no longer relevant, when the library was handed over to Aberdeen Public Library Reference Department in 1937.

Amendments to the constitution were approved sporadically in the inter-war years, for example, increasing the number of non-executive committee members from four to six in 1928 and a more extensive tidying-up revision in 1936. In 1939 a new "Associate" category of membership was created, intended for persons not normally resident in the vicinity of Aberdeen, but perhaps interested in receiving the exchange packet. There were applicants from Bournemouth, Blackpool and Linlithgow, but they were few in number and the category was abolished in 1952.

In 1954 a committee was appointed to consider the Society's constitution which was evidently seen as out of date. The committee took the view that "radical alterations" were required, "that the constitution be shortened, simplified and clarified" and it presented proposed amendments to the 1955 AGM. These were unanimously accepted and shortly after were published in a small booklet, including an Article allowing for Fellowships which had been approved in 1947 (see Ch. 16). The number of Articles were reduced from fourteen to ten by incorporation or elimination of some of the clauses, whilst what had previously been a separate set of Exchange Packet Rules became one Article of the constitution. An example of the way in which the constitution was updated in line with current practice was the elimination of any reference to standing committees, so that in future any sub-committees were *ad hoc* creations. One other way in which long-standing practice was recognised and formalised in the constitution was the statement that four Executive Officers were charged with the responsibility "for the day to day business of the Society". For some time past, the Treasurer, Secretary, President and senior Vice-President met at least once a year to "purge the membership roll", usually for non-payment of subscriptions, and to finalise the syllabus.

Two years later, in 1957, the number of non-executive committee members were reduced from six to five, and the delegate to the Association of Scottish Philatelic Societies (previously an informal office) was added to the Management Committee. This was a short-lived amendment, as these decisions were rescinded for no stated reason in 1959. By 1968 it was felt that the Management Committee was "rather unwieldy" and four of the office bearers, the Convener of the Expert Committee, Exchange Packet Secretary, Junior Section Representative and the Superintendent of Permanent Exhibitions were removed from *ex-officio* membership of the Committee, whilst non-executive members were reduced from six to four. This amendment seems to have resulted in further consideration of the constitution by the Committee and a revised draft was approved by the AGM of 1969. This was circulated in another small booklet in an edition of no less than 500 copies. The only major change was the elimination of the Article previously headed "Expert Committee". Otherwise, it incorporates a clear statement of the composition of the Management Committee as revised in the year previous, some minor rephrasing and it was set in a larger, more legible typescript.

Subsequently, there were changes to offices outwith the Management Committee. The post of Press Officer was combined with the Secretary's duties in 1978 and the Superintendent of Permanent Exhibitions was abolished in 1983. On the other hand, a tendency to create offices not specified in the constitution became apparent, with the creation of an Auction Secretary in 1979 and a Newsletter Editor in 1981. These functions had previously been fulfilled by members not formally elected to the posts. In 1986 the post of Press and Publicity Officer was resurrected.

At the 1996 AGM it was suggested that the constitution once again required revision because of recent changes in the activities of the Society. A copy of the existing constitution was circulated to all members inviting comment and with none forthcoming, the Treasurer and Secretary prepared a revised draft which the Committee approved. The revised draft was also circulated to all members and approved at the AGM of 1997 with minor amendments. The new constitution was drafted in non-gender specific terminology and incorporated an up-to-date list of posts, with the Committee empowered to co-opt into vacant posts. The membership of the Committee was clarified, the Article previously dealing with the Exchange Packet revised to match the current situation of a Room Packet and an Article introduced dealing with the Postal Auction. Despite slight enlargement, the new constitution could be printed out as required on two sides of A4 paper.

A proposal in 2000 that non-executive members of the Committee should be elected for a period of two years, rather than annually, was not ratified by any subsequent AGM, but it has sometimes happened that in a year when there is no change of President, a motion to re-elect the entire Committee has been approved, thereby hastening the business of the meeting! Then, in 2001, the Fellows of the Society were invited to review the bye-laws governing election to Fellowship and to make recommendations, bearing in mind that no elections to Fellowship had been made for twelve years and that the number of members was now lower than at the time when the institution of Fellowship was initiated. They decided that the proportion by which the number of Fellows should not exceed the total membership of the Society should be raised from 5% to 10%. The status of the Fellowship bye-laws was not clear, as there was no constitutional provision for them. The six bye-laws, dated 1955, are set out in a document signed by the then President and Secretary, neither of whom were Fellows, under a preamble reading "the undernoted guiding principles shall be observed". In any event, it was the Fellows who took the decision to increase the proportion to 10%, and they reported accordingly to the 2001 AGM. The current constitution requires the AGM to elect a Fellowship Awards Committee of three Fellows but this has not always happened in the present more relaxed and occasionally cavalier attitude towards constitutional affairs.

There has been one further revision of the constitution. This came about in consequence of an application to Awards for All Scotland for financial assistance in publishing this centenary history. An application was submitted in September 2008 but was ruled ineligible because of two clauses in the constitution, one of which was interpreted to mean that the Society was not open to all. The offending clause, which was in the original constitution of 1910, made provision for applicants to be excluded by three adverse votes. The other objection was the absence of any appeals mechanism against an expulsion procedure.

The 1997 constitution made no provision for an extraordinary general meeting so it was not possible to amend the constitution before the AGM of 2009. This proved to be fortunate in that there was, perforce, ample time for careful consideration and wide consultation. The committee set up a small working group of four to examine the existing constitution and to make recommendations. The group recognised an opportunity to modernise the constitution in respect of both terminology and content, not only to satisfy the reasonable requirements of grant awarding bodies in the twenty-first century, but also to rectify apparent omissions. The group set about rewriting the constitution in a way which would allow the Society to continue to operate without any obvious changes to its current procedures and practices, but within a more appropriate and clearly defined constitutional framework. Perhaps most significant was the absence of a clear statement that the Society was a non-profit distributing body and also the absence of any provision for dissolution. Also, the rules for the operation of functions such as the library were removed as Articles of the constitution, reverting to the pattern of the very first constitution. The draft proposals, which could still be contained on two sides of A4, were discussed, amended and approved by the committee and then circulated to all of the members in advance of the 2009 AGM, when the new constitution was unanimously adopted.

Article 1 of the constitution as originally approved reads: The Society shall be known as "The Aberdeen and North of Scotland Philatelic Society". In 1952 a past President gave notice of a motion to the forthcoming AGM, to change the title of the Society to the Aberdeen Philatelic Society, but the motion was withdrawn. Then, in 1967, a proposal that the name of the Society should be changed was referred to the Committee which decided to leave the name as it was. In 1997, however, a proposal to change the name of the Society to "The Aberdeen Philatelic Society" was agreed unanimously, on the grounds that there were now other philatelic societies in the north of Scotland and that our membership was not as widespread as was implied.

Chapter 19

Office Bearers: Years of Service

The original constitution of the Society created four Executive Officers, with two of these, Secretary and Treasurer, combined in one office bearer for the first two years. The current constitution names thirteen offices: President, three Vice-Presidents (Senior, Junior and Immediate-Past), Secretary, Treasurer, Curator of the Forgery Collection, Librarian, Packet Secretary, ASPS Delegate, Newsletter Editor, Postal Auction Secretary and Publicity Officer. A further four posts, Curator of Permanent Collections, Editor, Permanent Exhibition Supervisor and Superintendent of the Junior Section were created and abolished in the interim.

The following lists of office holders include only those who were formally appointed at AGMs, although some of the functions were carried out by members or holders of other offices before the formal recognition of the posts. For example, the Newsletter had been compiled regularly by the Publicity Officer and Secretary since 1966, some fifteen years before a dedicated Newsletter Editor was appointed. Similarly, the Delegate to the Association of Scottish Philatelic Societies (sometimes known as Congress Delegate) and the Postal Auction Secretary were posts created in recognition of a pre-existing function.

The first President of the Society remained in office for a decade before standing down. Throughout the inter-war years, some Presidents took office for only one year, whereas others remained in office for two or three years. From the 1950s, Presidents have normally been re-elected for a second year in office, thus serving a two-year term. Vice-Presidents frequently rise to the office of President but not always so. In the inter-war years, six Vice-Presidents did not become President; in some cases their election

144

may have been by way of recognition, rather than in any expectation of active involvement in the management of the Society.

The posts of Secretary and Treasurer are central to the well-being of the Society and probably carry the greatest work load. The twenty-one and twenty-two office bearers in each of these posts respectively have held office over very varying lengths of time, from short interim periods to decades of devoted service. The office of Forgery Curator is notable for long service, the original incumbent having held office for no less than forty-six years. By comparison, the offices of Superintendent of the Junior Section, Packet Secretary and Publicity Officer have seen greater turn-over, whilst the short-lived posts of Editor and Curator of the Permanent Collection both had the smallest possible number of office bearers! Functions have occasionally been fulfilled by more than one office bearer, e.g. Librarian and Superintendent of the Junior Section. A function may be abolished and then reinstated, e.g. Librarian and Publicity Officer, so the record of office bearers is not always continuous. Also, a member may have more than one period in a particular office, e.g. as Secretary or Librarian. The Treasurer's accounts are examined annually by Auditors, more recently Scrutineers and now Account Examiners. The manner of their appointment in the past is not always clear, although appropriate expertise was evidently relevant. Currently, they may be members of the Society but cannot also be committee members. The Society is grateful for their services.

Over the years, approximately 130 members have filled one or more of the various formal offices. Twelve members have been elected to five or more different posts during their membership of the Society. One has filled eight different posts. Another small cohort of members has loyally filled one chosen office for long periods, ten such members having filled one or more offices without interruption for at least a decade. The following lists use contemporary nomenclature, designations and abbreviations taken directly from the syllabus or from AGM minutes.

PRESIDENT

1910-20 James Anderson
1920-22 James M.A. Wood
1922-25 W. Edmund Bell
1925-26 Dr Peter Howie
1926-28 George Milne
1928-29 John Anderson
1929-30 W. Ferrier
1930-33 John Fraser
1933-35 George Beverley
1935-37 Dr A.D. Imper
1937-38 H.M. Wallace
1938-43 Dr V.M.M. Watson
1943-44 R. Dinnes
1944-45 W.J. Cramond
1945-47 Oswald A. Fraser
1947-48 Albert Smith
1948-49 E.W.S. Jupp
1949-51 Hector Monro
1951-53 J. Petrie
1953-55 G.D. Rae
1955-57 W.A. Fleming
1957-58 G.C. Skinner
1958-60 G. Robertson
1960-62 A.S. Mackie
1962-64 J.B. McKenzie
1964-65 G.L.Inglis
1965-67 J.J. Waterman
1967-69 G. McD. Mackintosh
1969-71 Mrs P.A. Orkin
1971-73 T.I. Baptie
1973-75 S. Miazek
1975-77 A. Black
1977-79 Capt. J.E.R. Thompson

VICE-PRESIDENT

1910-20 P.J. Anderson
1920-22 W. Edmund Bell
1922-24 George Milne
1924-25 Peter Howie
1925-26 George Milne
1926-28 John Anderson
1928-29 W. Ferrier
1928-33 Dr J.H. Stephen
1929-30 John Fraser
1929-32 Wm. Marshall
1933-34 R.W. Sherrit
1933-34 James Shand
1934-37 W.A. Fleming
1934-35 Dr A.D. Imper
1934-36 J.M. Stephen
1935-38 W.J. Cramond
1936-37 H.M. Wallace
1937-38 Dr V.M.M. Watson
1937-40 Hector Monro
1938-43 R. Dinnes
1941-44 W.J. Cramond
1943-47 E.J. Cooper
1944-45 O.A. Fraser
1945-47 Albert Smith
1947-48 E.W.S Jupp
1947-49 W.L. Falconer
1948-51 J. Petrie
1949-50 Chas. W. Hornal
1950-53 George D. Rae
1951-52 Chas. Hornal
1952-55 W.A. Fleming
1953-57 G.C. Skinner
1955-58 G. Robertson

1979-81 J. Malcolm

1981-83 Bruce Walker

1983-85 J.C. Stone

1985-87 J. Hannah

1987-89 A.L. Walker

1989-91 R.Λ. Stables

1991-93 D.A. Macdonald

1993-95 A. Finnie

1995-97 P.L. Payne

1997-98 J.J. Ritchie

1998-00 A.D. Kindley

2000-02 Mrs J. Thrower

2002-04 D. Graham

2004-06 J.R. Little

2006-08 E. Vase

2008- G. Stephen

1957-60 A.S. Mackie

1958-59 J.D. Davidson

1960-61 W.L. Falconer

1960-62 J.B. McKenzie

1961-62 A.F.L. McGregor

1962-64 G.L. Inglis

1962-65 J.J. Waterman

1964-65 A.W. Haig

1965-67 G. McD. Mackintosh

1965-69 Mrs P.A. Orkin

1967-68 J. Peter

1968-69 D. Edwards

1969-71 T.I. Baptie

1969-73 S. Miazek

1971-75 A. Black

1973-74 A.F.L. McGregor

1974-77 J.E.R. Thompson

1975-79 J. Malcolm

1977-81 B. Walker

1979-83 J.C. Stone

1981-85 J. Hannah

1983-87 A.L. Walker

1985-89 R.A. Stables

1987-91 D.A. Macdonald

1989-93 A. Finnie

1991-95 P.L. Payne

1993-95 Mrs S Den

1995-97 J.J. Ritchie

1995-98 A.D. Kindley

1997-00 Mrs J. Thrower

1998-02 D. Graham

2000-04 J.R. Little

2002-06 E. Vase

2004-08 G. Stephen

2006-10 A.D. Kindley

2008- M.F. Longhurst

SECRETARY

1910-12 Edward Alexander
1912-20 W. Edmund Bell
1920-22 George Milne
1922-26 John Alexander
1926-29 W.A. Fleming
1929-31 Hector Monro
1931-34 J.M. Stephen
1934-37 H.M. Wallace
1937-42 E.W.S. Jupp
1942-46 Albert Smith
1946-47 E.W.S. Jupp
1947-51 George Robertson
1951-53 J.D. Davidson
1953-55 Geo. Robertson
1955-57 Ian Smillie
1957-64 J.A. Wood
1964-70 J.B. McKenzie
1970-73 Bruce Walker
1973-90 J.T. Gawthorpe
1990-95 J.J. Waterman
1995-   Mrs S. Den

TREASURER

1910-12 Edward Alexander
1912-13 Hubert Mountfort
1913-14 Mrs Mountfort
1914-28 A. Gordon Smart
1928-32 R.W. Sherrit
1932-36 Wm. J. Cramond
1936-37 E.W.S. Jupp
1937-38 E.H. Shirran
1938-43 O.A. Fraser
1943-47 W.L. Falconer
1947-49 George D. Rae
1949-57 Alistair H. Beattie
1957-62 A.F.L. McGregor
1962-70 T.I. Baptie
1970-72 J. Bruce Adam
1972-75 G.L. Inglis
1975-76 B. Walker
1976-78 J.C. Stone
1978-82 I.B. Kennaway
1982-85 D. Clark
1985-08 N. Lutwyche
2008-   D.A. Macdonald

CURATOR OF THE FORGERY COLLECTION

1911-57 George Milne
1957-63 Dr V.M.M. Watson
1963-65 E. Reid
1965-69 Geo. Jaffray
1969-77 E.W.S. Jupp
1977-79 D.J.M. Kerr
1979-85 J.J. Waterman

LIBRARIAN

1910-12 W. Edmund Bell
1912-15 George Milne
1915-21 John Anderson
1921-22 James M. Benton
1922-26 James Shand
1926-28 J.I. Massie
1928-32 F. Forrest

148

1985-86 Nigel H. Trewin	1929-31 J.M. Stephen
1986-92 J.J. Waterman	1931-36 Edwin Reid
1992- A.L. Walker	1936-38 J.F. Cruickshank
	1965-74 J.J. Waterman
	1974-79 J. Malcolm
	1979-85 A.L. Walker
CURATOR OF PERMANENT	1985-90 R. Robson
COLLECTION	1990- A.L. Walker
1921-23 James Anderson	

PACKET SECRETARY	SUPERINTENDENT OF JUNIOR SECTION
1911-12 Alex. Milne	1920-28 John Fraser
1912-15 John Anderson	1925-28 Eric Duncan
1915-18 Geo. Milne	1925-28 Alan Fraser
1918-22 Alf. G. Weir	1928-31 Wm. Marshall
1922-26 James M. Benton	1931-32 W. Edmund Bell
1926-31 John Fraser	1932-33 R. Findlay Crabb
1931-33 Hector Monro	1933-34 John Anderson
1933-46 Dr. A.D. Imper	1934-35 John Fraser
1946-49 W.L. Falconer	1935-37 H.M. Wallace
1945-56 George D. Rae	1937-39 Hector Monro
1956-63 George Paterson	1939-40 R. Dinnes
1963-66 R. Dinnes	1945-46 W.L. Falconer
1966-67 Geo. Robertson	1946-50 Dr V.M.M. Watson
1967-69 Rev. J.G. Grant-Fleming	1950-54 J.B. McKenzie
1969-70 G. Alexander	1954-55 Miss M.B. Williamson
1970-73 J. Malcolm	1955-56 J.B. Mackenzie
1973-77 J.R. Little	1956-58 Dr V.M.M. Watson
1978-80 B. Walker	1958-61 A.H. Beattie
1980-82 Mrs E. Parsons	1961-63 Fergus C. Davidson
1982-84 I.B. Kennaway	1963-66 G. McD. Mackintosh
1984-95 John Clark	1966-67 Ian Smillie
1995-02 T.L. Beedie	1967-72 J. Malcolm
2002- A.G. Wilson	

PRESS & PUBLICITY OFFICER

1921-22 James M. Benton
1922-25 Athol D. Thomson
1925-26 George Ross
1926-27 Lindsay B. Duff
1927-28 R.W. Sherrit
1928-29 J. Ruegg
1929-30 Hector Monro
1930-33 George Beverley
1933-38 W. Edmund Bell
1938-43 T.W. Murray
1946-47 Albert Smith
1947-48 Hector Monro
1948-49 J. Petrie
1949-50 Albert Smith
1950-52 A.S. Mackie
1952-53 George Robertson
1953-63 E.W.S. Jupp
1963-65 G.L. Inglis
1965-67 Ian Smillie
1967-69 E.J. Fair
1969-72 Geo. I. Inglis
1972-74 A.F.L. McGregor
1974-78 J.T. Gawthorpe
1987-90 Bruce Walker
1990-91 N. Lutwyche
1991-95 Mrs. S. Den
1995-07 A. Finnie
2008-   F.C Jefferies

PERMANENT EXHIBITIONS SUPERINTENDENT

1933-37 James Shand
1937-39 Dr V.M.M. Watson
1939-40 H. Monro
1944-46 W.L. Falconer
1946-51 W.A. Fleming
1951-53 E.W.S. Jupp
1953-55 J.A. Ross
1955-59 A.S. Mackie
1959-63 L.B. Duff
1963-68 G. McD. Mackintosh
1968-69 Bruce Walker
1969-71 Miss D. Iball
1971-74 Mrs M. Malcolm
1974-76 Mrs E. Carroll
1976-77 J.B. McKenzie
1978-81 S. Miazek
1981-83 G. Gillespie

ASPS DELEGATE

1958-59 H. Monro
1959-70 J.A. Wood
1970-75 Geo. L. Inglis
1975-76 B. Walker
1976-77 Geo. L. Inglis
1977-87 G. McD. Mackintosh
1987-   J.C. Stone

POSTAL AUCTION SECRETARY NEWSLETTER EDITOR

1979-80 J.C. Stone
1980-81 Dr R.G. Evans
1981-90 N. Lutwyche
1990-96 J.J. Ritchie
1996-07 F.C. Jefferies
2007-08 A. Simmers
2008-   M.F. Longhurst

1981-84 Kenneth Taylor
1984-86 Nigel H. Trewin
1986-   J.C. Stone

EDITOR
1915-16 John Thomson

The office bearers and committee for the Silver Jubilee year 1935-36; from left to right, front row: W.E. Bell, John Fraser, Mrs Stevenson, H.M. Wallace, A.D. Imper, W.J Cramond, Geo. Beverley, Geo. Milne; back row: J.M. Stephen, W.A. Fleming, Jas. Boyd, Robt. Dinnes, C.A. Wilson, Ed. Shirran, Alex. Emslie, E. Reid, Jas. Scott.

George Milne.

22-4-1881 - 31-7-1957.

The Creator of this Forgery Collection and
its diligent Curator from the date of
its inception in 1910 until the
date of his death in 1957.

Appendix

Some Publications by Members

Anderson, John, 1929, *Scots Local Cancellations*, H.F. Johnson, London, pp.35.

Anderson, John, MBE, 1950, Scots Local Cancellations, [in] *ANSPEX HANDBOOK*, Aberdeen & North of Scotland Philatelic Society, 23-30.

Anderson, P.J., 1911, Notes on Early Philatelic Literature, *Stamp Collectors' Fortnightly* xvii, 178-181.

Anderson, P.J. & Smith, B.T.K., 1912, *Early English Philatelic Literature, 1862-65*, London.

Anderson, P.J., 1919, *Philatelic Literature Collecting in 1864-79. Reminiscences and Extracts from a Diary*, reprinted from the Journal of the Philatelic Literature Society XI, 1918, privately printed in a numbered edition of 30 copies, pp.47.

Anderson, P.J., 1923, Aberdeen Postage Stamps, 1867-68, *The Philatelist* 1, 3.

Anderson, P.J., 1923, Scottish Philatelic Literature 1867-1923, *The Philatelist* 1, 8:5-14, 9:5-7 & 10:3-4.

[Anderson, P.J.], 1923, *Second Rough List of Specimens of Philatelic Literature from the Aberdeen University Library*, Aberdeen University Press, edn. of 100 copies, pp.48.

ANSPEX Handbook, 1950, Aberdeen & North of Scotland Philatelic Society, Aberdeen, pp.64.

Bell, Edmund, W., 1931, *Exhibition of Stamps*, privately printed in an numbered edition of 75.

Collie, F. 1923, Fifty Years as a Philatelist, *Stamp Collecting*, 7 April, 7.

Daynes, John & Lutwyche, Nigel, 2006, *West African Forces Air Mail Letter Cards, Air letters & Honours Envelopes 1942-1945*, West Africa Study Circle & Forces Postal History Society, pp.31.

Duncan, Stewart P. & Andrew, Oliver, 2005, *The Postal Markings of the Gambia 1858 to 2000*, West African Study Circle, pp.144.

Falconer, W.L., 1950, A Short Postal History of Aberdeen, [in] *ANSPEX HANDBOOK*, Aberdeen & North of Scotland Philatelic Society, 43-51; [in] *The Northeast of Scotland A Philatelic Miscellany*, [ed. Jeffrey C Stone], Aberdeen & North of Scotland Philatelic Society, 1985, 3-10.

Fleming, W.A., 1950, "The Postal"...the Down Special T.P.O., [in] *ANSPEX HANDBOOK*, Aberdeen & North of Scotland Philatelic Society, 35-40.

Hannah, J., Mackie, A.S., Rosenblat, D.G., 1968, 2 Cents Admirals (First Issue), *Maple Leaves* 12, 8, 210-213.

Hornal, Charles, 1950, G.B. Cancelled in Aden An interesting problem, [in] *ANSPEX HANDBOOK*, Aberdeen & North of Scotland Philatelic Society, 7-8.

Kyle, James, 1973, Ocean Island, *Gibbons Stamp Monthly*, December.

Kyle, James, 1974, Posts of the Phoenix Group, *Gibbons Stamp Monthly*, May.

Kyle, James, 1975, Posts of the Line Islands, *Gibbons Stamp Monthly*, June.

Kyle, James, 1976, Cayman Islands – The early posts and first postage stamps, *Gibbons Stamp Monthly*, July.

Kyle, James, 1977, Cayman Islands "Scandal": The provisional issues of 1907-08, *Gibbons Stamp Monthly*, February.

Kyle, James, 1977, Tuvalu – Postal History of the Ellice Islands, *Gibbons Stamp Monthly*, May.

Kyle, James, 1978, The Union Group (Tokelau Islands), *Gibbons Stamp Monthly*, January.

Kyle, James, 1979, The Gilbert and Ellice Islands, *Gibbons Stamp Monthly*, June & July.

Lawrance, R. Murdoch, 1931, A Philatelic Souvenir, *Aberdeen Bon-Accord and Northern Pictorial*, 13 Feb.

Macdonald, David, 2003, *Denmark's Fri-Correspondance Kort*, David Macdonald, Aberdeen, pp.44.

Mackie, A.S., 1999, Some Aspects of the Rural Mail Delivery Service, *Maple Leaves* 26, 3, 105-110.

Milne, George, 1910, Line-Engraved, Lithographed, and Surface-Printed Stamps, *Stamp Collectors' Fortnightly* xvi, 214-215.

Milne, George, 1911, The Sunshine of Philately: A Study of Stamp Colours, *Stamp Collectors' Fortnightly* xviii, 11-13, 20 & 21.

Milne, George, 1912, The Picture Gallery of Philately, *Stamp Collectors' Fortnightly* xviii, 230 & 231, 239 & 240.

Milne, George, 1916, Lettering in Philately, *Stamp Collectors' Fortnightly* xxiv, 15, 106.

Milne, George, 1920, *Heraldry in Philately*, The Philatelic Institute, London, pp.66.

Milne, George, 1924, The Lithographic Process in Stamp Production, *Stamp Collectors' Fortnightly* XXX, 335-339.

Milne, George, 1924, How Postage Stamps are Printed. A Wireless Talk given from 2BD: The Aberdeen Station of the British Broadcasting Company on Wed. 30 January 1924, *Philatelic Magazine,* 103-105.

Milne, George, 1935, *Forgeries*, revised manuscript of a paper by the Expert and Curator of the Forgery Collection, Aberdeen PS archives.

Milne, George, 1950, Heraldry in Philately, [in] *ANSPEX HANDBOOK*, Aberdeen & North of Scotland Philatelic Society, 9-19.

Stables, R.A., 1985, Recorded Use of Scots Local Namestamps in Aberdeenshire and Kincardineshire 1840-1860, [in] *The Northeast of Scotland A Philatelic Miscellany*, [ed. Jeffrey C Stone], Aberdeen & North of Scotland Philatelic Society, 39-57.

Stables, Ron [Ed.], 1995, *Postal Markings of Scotland to 1840*, 2nd Edition, Scottish Postal History Society, pp.198.

Stables, R., 1982, The Implementation of the Additional Halfpenny Mail Tax at Edinburgh, *The Scottish Post*, 153-6.

Stables, R. & N. Trewin, 1983, The Birth and Death of the Scots Local Namestamp, *The Scottish Post*, 198-200.

Stables, R., 1986, The Scottish Postal Surveyors 1760-1840, *The Scottish Post* 31, 129-131.

Stables, R., 1989, The Aberdeen Penny Post Services 1824-1840, *The Scottish Post* 42, 262-70.

Stables, R., 1995, The Later 'Additional Halfpenny' Handstamps, *The Scottish Post* 68, 666-68 & 676-78.

Stables, R., 1998, Dundee: The Dotted Circle Datestamps, *The Scottish Post* 77, 863-7.

Stables, R., 1998, Greenock: The Dotted Circle Datestamps, *The Scottish Post* 80, 921-4.

Stables, R., 1999, Victorian Dumb Cancellations, *The Scottish Post* 83, 980-2.

Stables, R., 1999, The Single Pillar Stamps of Edinburgh, *The Scottish Post* 84, 1004-7.

Stewart, Col. A.E., 1933, Stamps of Sind - The Sind Daks, *Philately in Scotland* 1, 18, 332-3.

Stone, J.C., 1985, P.J. Anderson - Philatelic Archaeologist and Bibliographer, [in] *The Northeast of Scotland A Philatelic Miscellany*, [ed. Jeffrey C Stone], Aberdeen & North of Scotland Philatelic Society, 58-63.

Stone, Jeffrey C. (ed.), 1985, *The Northeast of Scotland: a philatelic Miscellany*, Aberdeen & North of Scotland Philatelic Society, Aberdeen, pp.63.

Stone, Jeffrey, 2006, The Dispersal of Agathon Fabergé's Great Collections, *The London Philatelist* 115, 198-210.

Tahl, Harry, 1925, *Notes on Line Engraved British Stamps*, Aberdeen & North of Scotland Philatelic Society, Aberdeen, pp.14, edn. of 100 copies.

Tchilinghirian, S.D. & Stephen, W.S.E. *Austrian Post Offices Abroad*, 6 vols., Austrian Stamp Club, 1964.

Tchilinghirian, S.D. & Stephen, W.S.E. *Stamps of the Russian Empire Used Abroad*, 7 vols., British Society of Russian Philately, 1957.

Thomson, John, 1911-1913, Philatelic Frivolities, [50 poems in] *Aberdeen Bon Accord* [photo of author p.13]

Trewin, N. *et al*, 1984, Aberdeen: The '1844' Type Numeral Handstamps, *The Scottish Post* 21, 3-5.

Trewin, N. *et al*, 1985, Aberdeen Mileage Marks 1808-1827, *The Scottish Post* 25, 55-6.

Walker, B., 1986, City of Aberdeen Post Offices, *Scottish Post* 26, 70-1.

Walker, B., 1995, Manuscript Cancellations of Aberdeenshire, *The Scottish Post* 65, 636-7.

Waterman, J.J., 1985, Grampian Mail by Rail, [in] *The Northeast of Scotland A Philatelic Miscellany*, [ed. Jeffrey C Stone], Aberdeen & North of Scotland Philatelic Society, 23-38.

Waterman, J.J., 1996, Aberdeen: Public Counter Datestamps with Identifying Letters, *The Scottish Post* 72, 767-9.

Waterman, J.J., 1997, The Down Special TPO: An Early Version in 1872, *The Scottish Post* 73, 775-80.

Waterman, J.J., 1998, Strathspey Mails: The Role of the GNSR, *The Scottish Post* 77, 78 & 80, 855-62, 879-88 & 916.

Waterman, J.J., 1999, Aberdeen Head Post Office: The Crown Street Premises of 1907, *The Scottish Post* 81, 936-42.

Watson, Dr. V.M.M., 1985, The ABC of Forgery Detection, [in] *ANSPEX HANDBOOK*, Aberdeen & North of Scotland Philatelic Society, 53-59.

The British Philatelic Trust – still a mystery

While most collectors have heard of the British Philatelic Trust, its role and purpose still remains a mystery to many.

To summarise the background, the Trust was established from surplus monies gathered to cover the costs of running the international stamp exhibitions held in London in 1980 and 1990. These monies were raised by the British Post Office through the surcharge added to a series of miniature sheets. Soon after its formation the Trust became a registered charity, and had to declare its objectives very clearly. These embrace the study, research and knowledge of postage stamps and postal history.

All actions by the Trust have to be approved by its Board of Trustees, embracing representatives of the philatelic world, the British Post Office, and others whose expertise is valued. The Trustees are accountable not only to the philatelic community but also to the Charity Commissioners. A few years ago the Trust came under the scrutiny of the Commissioners, and was found to be lax in some of the interpretations it was giving to its objectives. As a result it has had to be far more stringent in the way it views submissions for grants.

There are many who find it difficult to distinguish between the educational aspects of the study of stamps and postal history, and the encouragement of collecting. The Trust is not permitted to support the latter.

However, the Trust can support publications where the author has undertaken research and thereby is passing on this knowledge to others. Such research might be in the printed form, or could these days be available on-line. Help can be provided towards the actual research.

In this context, Trustees are actively examining ways in which they can help museums preserve essential records in digital form to make them more accessible to researchers.
Trustees are anxious to help libraries, particularly public libraries, if, by so doing, the knowledge of others can reach a wider audience.

Another way of reaching out is by exhibitions, and Trustees will look favourably at requests to help with the display of exhibits at exhibitions, especially when a wider audience can view the material. That is why the Trust is actively supporting many of the features of the next international stamp exhibition in London, London 2010 Festival of Stamps. The Trust also supports the Association of British Philatelic Societies in its endeavours to provide better exhibition display facilities.

Seminars and workshops can also aid the learning process, and again Trustees are willing to give financial support where appropriate.

The crucial point is that the Trust welcomes ideas. It has supported the distribution of this publication to a wider audience, appreciating that by so doing it meets with the Trust's objectives. Do not be afraid to put forward your ideas – one of the Trustees will be only too willing to help develop your thoughts if necessary. Simply write in the first instance to:

British Philatelic Trust,
Suite 101,
Business Design Centre,
52 Upper Street,
London N1 0QH.

159

Index

163

University of Stirling, 119
Uruguay, 16
USA, 16, 17, 22, 36, 46, 59, 72
USSR, 31
Utrecht, 130
Victoria Restaurant, 8
Vowles, L.T., 43
Walker Road Stamp Club, 57
Walker, Alex M., 95
Wallace, H.M., 151
War Comforts Co-ordination Committee, 41
War Loan, 134
War Savings Certificates, 133
War Stamps, 23
War Stock, 134
Warren, Frank, 96
Warren's *Pageant of Civilization*, 63
Washington, 59
Waterman, J.J., 119

Watson, Dr V.M.M., 19, 22, 32, 44, 102, 109
Wellsted, Raif, 22
West End Café, 85
West Indies, 22
Who's Who in Philately, 11
Wilde, P.A., 22, 32
Wilson, C.A., 151
Wilson, Charles, 14
Wilson, Sir John, 48
WIPA, 130
Wishart, Alan, 22
Wood, James, 121
Wright, H. & Creeke, A.B., *A History of the Adhesive Stamps of the British Isles*, 68
YMCA, 5, 6, 8, 32, 35, 37, 61, 62
Young, J. McLauchlan, 5, 60
Your Number is Up, 23
YWCA, 8, 33
Zanzibar, 22, 47